TABLE OF CONTENTS

THANKS TO MY FRIEND/SUDO-EDITOR, JAY DEAS. (AT this point all typos/mistakes are post-edit and are on me)

THANKS TO THE NURSES AT CHLA, BMT UNIT WHO CARED FOR MY CHILD AS I WROTE NEXT TO HIS BED FOR MONTHS

THANKS TO MY DOG LUCAS WHO SACRIFICED MANY WALKS AS I WROTE

YOU MIGHT NEED THIS:

my dad + Annie (my birth mother)= Kristen, James and me?

Jade (my step mother)+ 2 husbands prior to my dad = Max and Demi

Annie + Edgar (my dad's brother in law) = me?

Annie + Paul (boyfriend after dad)= Paulina

Annie + 4th father (some other man) = Geneva

Annie + 5th father (yet another guy)= Brandy

Sister Kristen: 14 when Jade & my dad married
Brother James: just turned 7 days before.
Step Sister Demi: 13 when they married
Step Brother Max: 15 when they married
I was just about to turn 5 when they married
and calling anyone my step brother or sister still
feels weird.

DEDICATION

This book is dedicated to my four men, my dad,
my husband and my two sons, Drew and
Bradley. However, it is dedicated especially to
my youngest son, Bradley, who has been
fighting a battle he didn't deserve since July
2018. Bradley deals in dignity, stoicism, and
grace while caring more about others than
himself. He is everyone's friend and is always
my biggest fan in every one of my endeavors.

A child can teach an adult three things:
To be happy for no reason
To always be curious
To fight tirelessly for something *-Paulo Coelho*

PREFACE

Our prime purpose in this life is to help others. And if you can't help them, at least don't hurt them.*-Dalai Lama*

For thirty years I wanted to tell this story but I was afraid. I didn't know why I couldn't write it or why I was afraid. Once I realized that not telling it was allowing it to have power over me and giving it permission to haunt me, I knew it was finally time.

Courage is knowing what not to fear*-Plato*

I started to understand I had been afraid to revisit certain memories, to expose certain truths and be accused of lying by people who had already discarded me many years before. I had to be sure my truth was absolutely accurate. What if my memory was skewed or tarnished? I needed to be fair, honest and kind.

I didn't and I don't want to hurt anyone. How could I possibly tell an ugly truth, mostly about someone I saw as a monster and do it kindly without hurting anyone? I couldn't think of a way. That's when my mother-in-law gave me a new best seller she thought I would like. It was 100,000 words I passionately devoured with a resonance I've never experienced before. The author's memories of her truth were reinforced by journals she had written over many years and she could compare them for accuracy. If her current memory matched what she had written in her journal decades before, then she could be confident what she was writing was truly truthful.

Memories are ambiguous and someone else will remember the same event differently but that's because they might have experienced it from a different perspective. I had to be okay with that. I started carefully writing from my heart. Several thousand words later, I started sleeping better. Nightmares of that house, dread, and fear stopped startling me awake in the middle of the night. I stopped waking in the morning feeling unrested and anxious as if I had made a punishable mistake.

A new peace came over me and I wanted to write more. I remembered a psychologist telling me eleven years before that I could move past this pain if I was willing to do the work. I finally understood that telling this truth was what she meant. I had thought, "Doing the work" meant something burdensome but this wasn't painful at all. Despite my optimistic visions of my book's outcome being a compelling page turner, I could also imagine the wrath that would follow from the characters raging "Lies, lies, lies!" I smiled at how silly that fear was because my writing had become so cathartic.

I was just beginning to experience a writer's high when out of nowhere I suddenly felt an unexpected recoil. I felt a very unforeseen epiphany that threw me back and took my heart and my mind by surprise. I had thought I was going to be writing about a sad and abusive childhood and a monster.

What makes a person a "monster" to me is having cruel intentions in which they have full knowledge of the harm they're causing, and commits their actions for no good cause, but rather their selfish desires.-*Alyah Scott*

Suddenly I didn't FEEL that was my entire truth. My memory of a monster who I felt had destroyed many lives began waxing and waning in my mind from someone simply with cruel intentions to a human being I had desperately loved as a child. I thought, "Wait! What's happening here? My childhood wasn't entirely bad after all. "I began to enjoy writing my story even more because joyful memories were emerging, not just bad ones.

I developed an even greater determination to respect those people with whom I shared these good memories and for whom I will always feel residual love. That's about when another shot fired in my psyche. The recoil this time left me sitting alone with the sadness and the painful memory I had subconsciously been avoiding. I was having to "do the dirty work." This one awful memory kept resurfacing as I wrote. My husband knew I was writing my story. At times when I was writing, he would have to pretend not to notice me crying because he knew I was doing the work and that I had to do it on my own. Around that time on this journey, the last thing I was expecting to find was a four leaf clover. But there it was. I was cleaning out some old dusty boxes in the garage when I found a familiar looking unlabelled book. It had a filigree heart on the cover. A tiny square hole was in the middle of the heart and I could see a butterfly through the square hole that represented a window. My left hand was already holding up the garbage can lid when I froze with my right hand extended like a selfie stick and stared at the book in my hand. Something made me stop, sit down in the middle of my driveway and open the book. I was surprised to see it dated 1998. Every page was covered with my handwriting. I was surprised to see that I had actually begun telling my story many years ago in this journal with my own handwriting and a date. The journal was almost verbatim to chapters I have written here twenty years later. A tender and supportive sensation of validation, maybe even self-love came over me. It felt like a warm blanket on a cold, wet day and I felt my heart swell because I knew my truth was THE truth. I became more motivated to organize the garage. I found more. I found folders full of love letters to and from old boyfriends that helped me go back in time. I found random journal entries dated from the 80's and 90's. What? I wrote about loving my family, wanting to live my best life and do good things. I had letters from people telling me what a good person I was and how much they WANTED to be in their lives. I saw myself as someone other than my family remembers and for the first time, I really liked her. I was after all always a good person and I had documentation, proof. I no longer needed someone else to justify it. Just like this other inspiring author had self-validation in her journals, and I felt empowered to keep going......

WHEN I FLY

Smell the sea and feel the sky, let your soul and spirit fly- *Van Morrison*

Late at night, while everyone else sleeps, I get up wearing crisp white cotton pajamas. Delighted and well rested, I go to the open window sill and step in. It's a beautiful, wide open window way up high with a breathtaking view. Maybe I'm in a lovely rustic hotel on the Amalfi coast cliffs or a Tuscan building on the top of a hill overlooking a vineyard. Sometimes, I can smell honeysuckles and freshly cut grass. On other nights, I breathe in the scent of the coming season of fall at the beach; my favorite. I spread my arms open wide and lean forward. I don't have to flap my arms rapidly like a bird to take flight. I begin to glide through the air freely. Like an eagle, I see everything clearly as I fly over the mountains and through the clouds. Comforting rain begins to fall as I whiz through the sky and it feels amazing. I'm always going to the same place, the ocean. I pull my arms back the way a torpedo gannet pulls back it's wings to dive for fish. Instead, I smoothly glide in at an angle to swim with the fish. We're always swimming in the same direction.

Sometimes, I swim with whales and I know we're going somewhere together. I don't know or care where we're going; it just feels purposeful and in toto. Sometimes, I swim with dolphins, giant rays or sea turtles. It's always beautiful, peaceful, serene. Vibrant and colorful fish swirl happily and freely near the top of the water. I glance down at the ocean floor and see flounder lying flat on the bottom. They shuffle around in the sand with their two eyes on the top of their flat bodies looking up at the rest of us. They don't long to be at the top of the water with the other fish because they have never known what that's like; their place is at the bottom. They are relatively content where they are. The flounder and I politely acknowledge each other like old friends as if I were a flounder in another life. I finish my visit with the creatures beneath the sea, I fly home and wake in the morning refreshed from the memories of my familiar flight. I never know which nights I will get to fly and sometimes I go months or even years between flights. However, the soul knows when it's time to fly and has been taking me there since I was a little girl. I expect that I'll continue these periodic flights of refuge for the rest of my life.

CHAPTER 1-ANNIE

My memory of her is blurry much like a dream from long ago yet I don't have the slightest recollection of her face. I specifically and only remember my last summer visit when I was five years old. She showed me a scar on the side of her abdomen and told me that her tummy was sliced open there so the doctors could pull me out. I looked for the scars where the doctors had pulled out my older brother and sister but I didn't see any and I didn't ask. I remember this scene like it was yesterday but I don't see her face in this memory or any for that matter. I've never seen a cesarean scar like that so I still don't know if I was actually born by c-section or if she made it up. I don't know why she would fabricate such a story unless it was for the same reason people tell children they were dropped off by a stork. Maybe she was preserving my innocence. This is one of so many questions I expect to go unanswered in this lifetime.

I remember sitting in her bathtub and gazing out the window. She poured Mr. Bubble under the tap until the tub was full and bubbly and then she disappeared. I stayed in the bathtub until my fingertips were raisins watching the next door neighbor chase chickens in his backyard. I thought the man was just playing tag with them in the way little children chase pigeons until he finally caught a chicken, swung it around by the neck and lopped off its head with something. Was it an ax? A machete? A knife? I was only five years old. I hadn't learned the difference between one tool or another so I suppose that's why I can't tell you exactly what it was. I can tell you, however, that the chicken ran around in circles with no head until it collapsed dead on the ground.

I don't know that I would have remembered the Mr. Bubble, the bath or the cesarean scar had it not been for the headless chicken running around the yard. The other memories are just caveats to the headless chicken which is the kind of thing a five year old doesn't forget.

She/Annie listened to Elvis Presley and Johnny Cash on a record player that was inside of a cabinet. It looked like a piece of brown furniture with a lid that propped up like the top of a baby grand piano. Inside the lid was the turntable where she played her albums. Lively music could often be heard throughout the house and I really liked it. I remember a feeling of freedom to sing and dance, so unconfined.

She had a boyfriend named Paul. They took me to a country night club and sat me up on the bar. Someone handed me a tambourine and I kicked and dangled my feet as I fancied I was part of the band. I watched the two of them dance the night away until my eyes grew heavy. Then I curled my little body into a ball in one of the booths and fell asleep. For years to follow, I remembered Paul as a man with a rooster's head because he came home drunk very early in the morning and woke us with a "cock-a-doodle-do." I also think he may have even climbed up on the fence because that's how I remember it; a man climbing up on a fence and crowing like a rooster as the sun came up.

I heard later that during their brief relationship, Annie and Paul had one daughter together. This was after she either gave my sister, brother and me away or after we were taken from her. I still don't know the real truth about that. They named their little girl Paulina after Paul. That would technically make her our half sister even though I would never know her.

On this same and final visit, Annie took my sister Kristen, my brother James and me to a church where they were healing people with potions and speaking in tongues. The service was outside in a wooded area where I stepped on a nail that traveled almost all the way through to the other side of my foot. Someone pulled the rusty nail out of my foot, poured some holy water on it, prayed and sent me on my way.
At five years old, I didn't know anything about tetanus shots and certainly didn't have the knowledge to be concerned about infection. I believed the holy water took care of it not only because they told me it would but it also seemed to heal with no problems whatsoever.

But why was the church service out in the woods? I wonder.Later that visit, my brother, James accidentally slammed the car door on my hand. The pain was so intense I felt frozen and couldn't speak; I wasn't able to tell anyone my hand was slammed in the door. I sat there paralyzed in my seat as Annie started the car and drove along to wherever we were going. It felt like an eternity before she realized my entire hand was inside the door. Most of my fingers were broken. They healed on their own albeit it appears I'm still slightly more "double jointed" in that hand than the other. I can still contort the fingers of that hand in ways that some people find disconcerting. I suppose it's from the way my bones had no choice but to heal on their own.

Another day on that same visit, my brother James and I were waiting for her in the car. Somehow we knocked the car out of park. The car rolled itself right out of the driveway and backwards down a hill. Some men came running toward the car and stopped it moments before we approached oncoming traffic at the bottom of the hill.

Was she negligent or just unlucky?

Can you imagine my dad and my new mom Jade's reaction when we came home and told them of our adventures? To us, they were adventures but to them these were reasons to take us away from Annie, forever. When we came home from that visit, my new mom, Jade said I wasn't going to visit my birth mother anymore. I'm not exactly sure and I'm only speculating but I can imagine that since my dad already had sole custody since I was a baby, Annie must have lost her visitation rights. In my mind, I can also imagine my new mother, Jade at court giving a persuasive and dramatic performance. There were probably enough reasons based on this trip alone to build a case against my birth mother. Jade was adept at producing tears on demand and may have used them in a convincing testimony that left everyone in dismay at my birth mother's neglect. I will never know the actual details; I can only imagine.

I didn't think through all of the moving parts because I was five, but I really didn't mind not seeing Annie again. I don't think I felt a strong connection to her. Or did I? I will never know.

My dad raised Kristen, James and me by himself since I was an infant. I don't know what the visitation arrangement was while I was a baby and a toddler. However, other than these few memories of my birth mother, I remember only being with my dad, my sister, and my brother. I can't speak for my dad but I believe my brother, sister and I were very, very happy. I have almost euphoric memories of our little red house on Lindenwood Drive. I remember snuggling with my dad while he fell asleep watching football on the weekends. I remember waking him up with incessant questions and him answering them patiently, sweetly, with never, ever a hint of irritation.

I remember a woodpecker drilling holes in a tree outside the open door. I asked my dad a million questions about why the woodpecker was drilling holes in the tree. He never showed any agitation whatsoever.

He was a single parent, a salesman, and so tired on the weekends yet had so much earnest love and patience. He was as close to perfect as I can ever imagine.

Then he met Jade who changed him and completely took over our lives and designed our destinies. I'm not saying she solely carried out our destinies but I am certainly saying that she designed them. Just like a fashion designer can design something the way he or she wants, how people decide to carry out those fashions will ultimately be up to them individually and independently....

Shortly after my dad married Jade and after that fateful visit to see my birth mother, Annie drove down from Alabama to pick us up for another visit. I was still only 5 years old and James was only 7. My new mom, Jade and my dad told us to stay inside the house when she arrived. We hid behind the fancy golden yellow tapestry curtains that came with the Jade package and watched from the window. They walked out to the driveway and exchanged words with my faceless birth mother, Annie. As she drove away, I don't remember how I felt but I knew for certain I wasn't going to see her again.

I don't know what James was feeling because we never spoke of it and I doubt we will ever speak again.

I wonder now how Jade and my dad felt at that moment. Did they feel validated because my birth mother, Annie was an unfit mother and they thought they were doing the right thing for us? Sadly, I doubt they felt compassion for her as she drove the eight hours back home without her children.

We were later told that my fourteen-year-old sister, Kristen refused to go on this trip and was hiding outside. Our next door neighbors had a peacock cage that attached to our fence and backed up to the sea wall of the canal. The canal ran between our backyard and the backyards of the people who lived on the next street over. Whenever one of the next door peacocks shed a beautiful long tail feather, I fished it out through the fence with a long stick or a tree branch. I would run inside and give the feather to Jade in hopes of earning her love. I don't have the slightest idea how she received my gifts and I don't remember feeling disappointed by her reaction. I also don't remember feeling as if I had endeared myself to her at all. Just nothing.

Now, to be fair and with love and compassion, was it my lack of understanding or was it her inability to show emotion or did she just not care? I don't think I have the right to pass that judgement. I can only tell you my truth as I remember it and I don't remember feeling any affection from Jade at all. Ivy covered the canal side of the peacock cage facing the sea wall. This made it difficult to see from the yard to the canal. This is where Kristen was later found on the cinder block wall teetering on her tip toes as she gripped her hands to the peacock cage. I don't know how long she had been hiding there and I never asked why she didn't want to go to Alabama. However, it made sense that my dad and my new mom didn't want little James and me to go to Alabama to visit Annie without Kristen to look after us.

I now think about that fourteen year old girl and I wonder why she didn't want to go. Had Jade said something to her to make her want to hide? Being at an age where she was more in tune with her feelings than I was, she must have felt awful and guilty. Knowing Jade the way I do, I can't imagine her offering Kristen any comfort after having made such a difficult decision.

This event changed the trajectory of our three lives and affected each of us in different yet monumental ways. I can't help but wonder how Kristen felt that day as she carried such a heavy weight and I will never know.

We were told not to ask questions and to forget about our birth mother because she was "no good". We were told we now had a new, better mom. My new mom, Jade forbade me to talk about my birth mother. I don't know why, but we often drove by a particular church with a large steeple. In the beginning, every time I saw that church, I blurted out "That's where my mommy goes to church." It was almost impulsive like I couldn't stop myself. I also don't have any idea why, but I remember believing this notion wholeheartedly which wasn't possible because we were in Florida and she was in Alabama. Jade would become very angry and glare at me with her cold green eyes.

Later, she would frighten me by saying, "If anyone other than me ever comes to pick you up from school, I need you to run and tell the teacher." In my mind, I pictured my birth mother as someone evil like Cruella de Vil in "101 Dalmatians" sending dreadful, cartoon-like kidnappers to steal me away from my new family. My vision of Annie became darker and darker as time went by.

When Jade first told me she was going to be my new mom, she stooped down and surveyed me. She shook her head dubiously and said, "But you're going to need a lot of work." She noted that my right ear stuck out like Dumbo. I didn't know who Dumbo was. She blamed it on my birth mother. She explained that when I was an infant, I was left in my crib alone for hours with my ear folded backwards against my head. She explained that people who loved their babies rolled them over so this wouldn't happen.

In a way, I felt sad for that little baby as if she were someone other than me. I then pictured myself as a silly, ugly baby just laying there too stupid to even cry out for help. I was embarrassed. I assumed I must have been an ugly baby because Jade told me that no one would come and visit the hospital when I was born. She explained that I was an unspeakable disgrace but she never explained why. I had never seen a baby picture of myself and later learned there were only two. One was a newborn picture in which my head was shaped like an egg which makes me question whether or not I was born by c-section. That baby's head looked like it struggled to come out of the birth canal. In the other picture I looked to be about six months old and I thought I looked sweet and cute in my pale yellow dress. I appeared to have a little bit of a twinkle in my eye like I imagined Santa had in "Twas the night before Christmas." I've always thought all babies were cute so I didn't think I was anything special. I just thought I was cute enough that someone could have loved me and I was slightly baffled as to why they didn't. Of course, I didn't ask any questions. I began to wonder but to never ask. For the first time, I now look at that picture differently. I see a happy little baby that someone cared enough about to put in a pretty little dress and have a professional photo taken. Someone was likely making me laugh and it was probably my brother or sister who probably dearly loved their baby sister. I also wonder if my birth mother may have had ulterior motives. Maybe she wanted to show someone the baby they were missing out on or maybe, just maybe she loved me the way moms love their babies. It's so hard to fathom, to know, because I'm now a mom and I just can't understand how she could go on living as if the three of us didn't exist.

When Jade brushed my hair back to put it in ponytails, the brush caught on my Dumbo ear which certainly didn't feel nice to me and irritated her. She began taping my ear to the side of my head so that it would grow without protruding. My new brother, Max who had come with the Jade package thought it would be funny to call me "Monkey." Not only because I carried around a stuffed purple and yellow monkey named Alfie but also because Max said my ear stuck out like Alfie's. It really wasn't that noticeable and he teased me lovingly. I liked my new nickname, I loved the attention and I really liked my new teenage brother who was almost ten years older than me.

Jade ingrained in my mind that my birth mother was worthless. She said I was pigeon toed from being neglected. She took me to a doctor who gave me big heavy shoes that looked like wingtips. I wore these type of orthopedic shoes for many years until my knees stopped knocking together when I walked.

She said I had rancid breath and took me to a dentist who extracted my abscessed teeth. Jade blamed my birth mother for my foul breath and rotten teeth. She explained that her daughter Demi didn't have a single cavity because she, as a responsible mother made sure her teeth were brushed properly.

I had recurring sinus infections and eventually had to have my tonsils removed. In the few childhood pictures that were taken of me, you can see that my eyes had dark circles underneath. I'm guessing this was due to unaddressed allergies. I specifically remember coughing and clearing my throat constantly. I remember looking around and wondering why other little girls didn't seem to have runny noses, sore throats or seem to have trouble getting enough air like I experienced on occasion. I had never heard of allergies, yet in hindsight, I suffered from them for many years. I even remember in eight grade math class, I sat behind a boy who had extremely short hair for ROTC. I spent the school year trying to cough quietly in my hand because he wiped the back of his bare neck every time I coughed as if I was coughing directly on him. Jade never seemed to notice. You might say, "Well what about your dad? He could have noticed." Maybe he could have and should have. However, in the deep south and in the 70's, those types of things were delegated to the mom. My dad worked long, hard hours and came home exhausted. I really admire the sacrifices he made to provide for us and understand why he didn't notice so many things. I also know that he is so incredibly sorry and that he loves us with all of his heart. Love forgives honest mistakes and that's the best explanation I can give.

Jade told me I was to never speak of Annie and if I ever agreed to see her I would be a traitor to my family. Why would she tell me this at an age when I had no control over whether I could see her or not? I believe she was forming my mind early on so that when I reached the age I could decide, I would not even consider. I believe she wanted me to know early on that my allegiance belonged to her. I didn't want to betray anyone, ever.

"Annie" and "my mommy" became dirty words and when I thought of her, I imagined a cock crowing and me as Peter betraying Jesus. I imagined this time and time again until thoughts of my birth mother dissolved completely. I didn't think about her anymore, not until I was eighteen years old when my older sister Kristen decided to tell me all about her. I'll tell you about that later.

CHAPTER 2-THE JADE PACKAGE

Some find it hard to believe but I somehow convinced myself that Jade was indeed my birth mother. People would say I must have inherited Jade's green eyes and others noticed I was left handed just like my "my mom." When we were alone, she told me my eyes were nothing like hers and that mine were actually yellow, not green. She always said this with a bad taste in her mouth. She pointed out that I was the only one in the family with yellow eyes and I didn't belong. She quizzed me, "Why is it that everyone else has blue or green eyes except for you? Why do you think that is?" I had no idea what she meant.

Skipping to my mid twenties for a moment, as soon as I could afford it, I bought green contacts to try and disguise my unfitting yellow eyes. I knew my eyes at least had a tint of green and I wanted desperately for them to be green like Jade's. I think I had an allergy to the contact material and didn't wear them for very long because it always felt as if someone was sticking their finger in my eye. I almost think this was fate trying to tell me to accept, maybe even love myself, yellow eyes and all. Coincidentally, many people over the years have told me that my eyes were beautiful, extraordinary. I couldn't hear them, I couldn't trust them, I couldn't believe them. Jade's voice overrode any and all compliments for decades. Instead, I could only hear Jade's voice reminding me that my eyes were ugly, that people only complimented me out of pity and that I didn't belong. It wasn't until 2018 when my own beautiful son at 12 years old grabbed my face as if seeing them for the first time and said, "Mom, your eyes are so cool. They are blue, green, and yellow. They're amazing," did I really believe it was true. And his opinion was all that mattered anymore.

I also had a tendency toward my left hand, yet I could use both. Once I realized that Jade was left handed, I stopped myself from using my right hand to eat or write all together. I needed to be left handed, like Jade, my "mom." I liked it when people thought she was my mother and I didn't feel dishonest for not explaining that she wasn't. It was easier than one might imagine for a little girl who wanted and needed a mother to convince herself of such a thing.

Jade was good to me in the beginning and she presented this family merger as a beautiful thing, just like "The Brady Bunch." She bought me dresses and let my hair grow long. People started to realize I was a little girl instead of mistaking me for a boy. I loved looking like a girl and no longer having to wear my brother's hand me down clothes.

CHAPTER 3-HOME IS HOME

Although the wind blows terribly here,
the moonlight also leaks between the roof
planks of this ruined house. *-Izumi Shikibu*

With the Jade package, we were able to move from our tiny little house in Panama City, Florida to what seemed like a great big brick house on a canal in a suburb called Lynn Haven. However, we (locals) consider Panama City and Lynn Haven one and the same.

When I speak of my hometown, I often describe it as practically Alabama because Panama City is in the panhandle of Florida and just as southern as one might imagine any small town in Alabama to be. Our family never traveled because it seemed to me that my Dad and Jade nor anyone else I knew had any need to see the rest of the world, except for me. Even for me, it was just a fantasy, way back then. I didn't know for sure that I was ever going anywhere. I suppose some people back home felt they already lived in Paradise and there wasn't a need to go anywhere else.

The beaches are literally so squeaky white they look like sugar. I grew up thinking that all beaches were white. I was surprised and disappointed twenty years later when I learned they aren't.

Panama City Beach is on the Gulf of Mexico where the clear blue water is home to dolphins jumping everywhere. On a recent visit, the stingray swam up to my ankles and then quickly darted away as if teasing me to chase them. I felt like a little girl back when we dove for sand dollars that were the size of salad plates and easily found giant conk shells.

We took our boat out to shell island where we found big horseshoe crabs. I thought they scary looking and fascinating at the same time. They reminded me of giant cock roaches in a shell. I would lie down prone in the shallow water near the shore with my mask on my face so I could dip my head under and watch the tiny seahorses clinging with their little tails to the sea grass; this was mesmerizing. Looking back, I realize that my personal memory has preserved this place as a sort of paradise. I've taken so much pleasure in watching my own children listen to my stories of what was almost every day to me as now something almost magical to them.

The backyard of our big, new house ended at a seawall where oysters grew. We could reach down and grab them if we wanted, although we never did. We actually spent more time trying not to get cut by them while fishing off the sea wall or getting in and out of various little boats we had acquired over the years. When the tide was high, on occasion, alligators floated up and sunned themselves in our yard. We were terrified of them even though all they really wanted was to sun themselves and well, gobble up our beloved beagle, Lady, bless her soul.

When I was really young, my new sister, (notice I don't say, "Step" sister) Demi told me there was a wicked witch that lived at the bottom of the canal. I never wondered how the witch breathed underwater. It sounded perfectly reasonable to me that a witch lived down below because Demi said she did. She said if the witch ever caught me alone near the canal she would turn me to stone. Demi had a great imagination about such things and I commend her for terrifying me with this idea. It kept me from cutting myself on the oyster shells or worse, falling in and drowning.

I was also afraid of the canal water because of the needle fish. She said they would swim through my knee caps leaving holes that would last forever.

I believed whatever Demi said and she took a great deal of pleasure in my naivety. Our front door was framed with holly trees and I loved pulling off the red berries and doing random things with them. Demi told me that if I pricked my finger with one of the pointy leaves, I would fall into a deep sleep forever like sleeping beauty. I never dared to touch them again for years. By the time I realized this was nonsense, I had grown out of the desire to pull off the berries anyway.

She mixed up concoctions in the blender consisting of pickles, ketchup, sardines, ice, and whatever else she felt like and told me it was the most delicious drink she ever had. I would drink it every time as she stood there satisfyingly smiling and encouraging me to finish it.

Demi showed me glass jars my dad kept in his closet. They looked like they were full of something you might scoop up from a dirty pond full of tadpoles. She said James and I had worms that lived inside our bums and that when we were asleep at night, our dad pulled them out and put them in these jars. I found this completely appalling yet it never occurred to me that he might have preferred to throw them out rather than keep them in a jar. I never once in my life ever asked him about the worms he pulled from our bums. However, forever and ever, and until now, I kept this horrid secret to myself. I had forgotten about that and many other such things because my adult life has brought me so much joy that overrides them. It wasn't until last year, my dad said, "Did you know that when you were little, I took up the hobby of brewing my own beer? I kept jars of brewing hops in the top of my bedroom closet." Ah-ha! At last, I remembered the worms and was so relieved to learn they were just beer hops after all.

Some bad things happened to Kristen, James and me after Jade came along but we also had some fun. We had bikes, dogs, cats, a pool table, a ping-pong table, roller skates and were not deprived of opportunities to have fun. We had a lot of fun and some really good times. I believe we all have good and bad memories. Despite the ratio of either/or, isn't it what we choose to do with them that matters? I choose to purge the bad ones by sharing them here in hopes to show others they are not alone and to bring awareness to mental and psychological abuse. As a caveat, this story is also intended to bring some awareness and understanding to inherent prejudice if even on a small scale. You'll read about that later.

CHAPTER 4-DUCKS, CIRCUS FREAKS & SIDE SHOWS

When I was nine years old, I practiced cartwheels perpetually until I reached the sea wall. That's where I heard pitiful, desperate quacking coming from the canal. To my surprise, it was a tiny lone yellow baby duck pacing back and forth against the seawall.

It was precious; like something you would find on an Easter card. It's teeny little feet paddled as fast as they could go. I had seen many baby ducks with their mothers before but they were always brown and never alone. I ran to the garage and grabbed a bucket. I laid down on the seawall quietly hovering the bucket above the baby duck. It took a while to catch it and the poor thing became even more desperate when it realized it was my prey. I felt so sad for the duck and I wondered if it missed its mother or if it knew it would never see her again. Finally, I scooped up my little prize in the bucket. I thought about my favorite game at the county fair which involved picking up a plastic duck as it floated by on a water covered conveyor belt. The attendant would then issue us a prize that corresponded to a number on the underside of the duck. It never failed that I always won a plastic Snoopy keychain year after year. Yet even the biggest prize of a giant stuffed bear could not have meant as much to me as did this tiny little life and I was determined to save it. No one was in the house except for the oldest of my two brothers, Max (notice that I don't say, "Step brother") who was home from college and he was sleeping. At the time, it seemed natural to run a bath for my duck and put him in the tub. He quacked and quacked and I couldn't quiet him. Max came storming into the bathroom and told me to remove the duck from the house or he would do it himself. I knew that ducklings need the warm feathers of their mother and fortunately, Mrs. Dejarnett who lived just down the street had an incubator. I anxiously ran to her house cupping the baby duck in my hands and put it in her incubator. Over the next year, we watched it grow into the most beautiful and also the first white duck I had ever seen.

It never occurred to me to go and look for that baby duck's mother. What if I had not removed it from the canal? Would she have come back for it? Is it actually my fault this duck was not reunited with its mother when I actually only wanted to save it? I wondered if this little duck was abandoned by its mother because it was yellow and didn't look like the others. Was it abandoned or was it there all alone for some other reason? There's not much data on why ducks abandon their ducklings but what I did find is that it's often not by a choice of the mother's. Sometimes they get separated on their first trip out of the nest looking for water or a predator spooks the ducks and they get split up.

I often wondered if I was like that baby duck. I wonder if my birth mother was metaphorically spooked away by a predator. Maybe I was purposely abandoned or found myself feeling alone for some other reason I can never understand. As human beings, I think we often assume orphaned children just weren't wanted by their parents. Most of us can't understand why a mother wouldn't want her babies and we judge without bothering to seek understanding. It's easier that way.

I don't know if Annie wanted us or not or if she just gave up fighting for us. As a mother, I just can't imagine giving up my children or giving up the fight for them.

When people hear about my current relationship with my family members, they question why I would ever go back. I try to explain that it's because it was a beautiful place. I have lovely memories mixed in with the bad ones and I have people who I love that still live there. I'm sure many other people have similar feelings about their hometowns. Home is home.

If you're not from a small southern town that has a county fair, it's just impossible to know what its like. The county fair brings out everyone from everywhere; people who seem to go nowhere else other than the county fair. Every year, my dad had a tent where he offered free hearing tests so my brother James, sister, Kristen and I spent a great deal of time there. I don't remember Demi or Max ever going with us to the fair. It certainly wasn't the most refined venue. However, I loved being with my dad while he tested people's hearing, playing pick up ducks and eating cotton candy.

The county fair tried to mimic the circus by offering up circus freak animals. I specifically remember seeing the five legged cow. I was only seven years old when I noticed a cow that had an extra leg. I could see the stitches where someone had sewn on an extra leg to this poor cow as spectators gathered around in awe.

I wanted to scream out to the crowd "Can't you see where they sewed on an extra leg?" But of course, I didn't. I wasn't allowed and never dared to speak my mind. I also remember a "neanderthal man" frozen in ice. We were charged a fee to view him. I thought to myself, "Why don't we just thaw him out to see what he really looks like?" It never occurred to me that if he was a real neanderthal man, he might be studied in a scientific lab or displayed in a reputable museum rather than a county fair in Panama City, Florida. But you see, it was visceral. This kind of entertainment had started with P.T. Barnum in the 1800s when he paraded Joyce Heff around as a 161 year old former maid to George Washington. When she died, the autopsy showed that she was only 80 years old but no one cared. They wanted to believe someone could live that long just like we wanted to believe the cow had five legs and that we were really observing a neanderthal man! We were willing to accept nonsense in the presentation of a curiosity as long as it was entertaining. Yet I still felt sorry for that cow in the same way I pitied the circus freaks when the circus came to town. I felt sorry for them the way that I felt sad for African Americans, interracial couples and anyone who wasn't heterosexual. It disturbed me to see people with deformities not just because they were hard to look at but because I didn't feel we should be paying money to stare at them when I had been taught not to stare. It seemed to me that everyone else saw it as harmless entertainment while I saw it as exploitation. Something deep inside me wanted them to go and play and be happy rather than travel from town to town as a gruesome spectacle to behold. It felt as if I could see and feel their sadness. Freaks and side shows eventually faded out of the circus because of this very reason. However, it turns out many of those very people did not feel exploited. They had jobs, friends, families and an income. Some of these "circus freaks" with physical deformities didn't mind being paid to be stared at. It was normal for them like its normal for a flounder to have two eyes on the top side of its body. I went to the county fare and the circus and enjoyed it just like everyone else except I always felt somewhat conflicted by injustice. Even the fat lady. I wondered if they gorged her with pies all day to make her fat. By now she would be out of a job anyway because well, she wouldn't be so unique these days, now would she?

Jade signed me up for kindergarten and I absolutely couldn't wait to go to school. Once we arrived, I clung to Jade's long legs until Mrs. Kristo gently and encouragingly pried me away. I could see tears in Jade's eyes and I felt a little happy at the thought that she was going to miss me. It was my first perceived bonding moment with Jade and I believed with all my heart that those tears meant she was going to love me.

That's where I met Roosevelt. He was my first black friend and I adored him. He was just Roosevelt and he wasn't black or white to me. He was just Rosie and sometimes Roosevelt. He didn't care which one.

One weekend early in my kindergarten year, our new family of seven went to a store to buy some more furniture for our new house. I was thrilled to find Rosie happily riding a rocking horse in the store window. His face lit up and we waved to each other frantically the way five-year-olds do when they realize each other exists outside of school.

My siblings teased me on the drive home and for days after about Roosevelt because he was black. They sang "Kathy and Rosie sitting in a tree, K-I-S-S-I-N-G". They weren't just teasing me about a boy. They teased with mirth at the sheer idea of a white girl with a black boy. The teasing was endless. They sang "three little (N-words) lying in the bed, one rolled over and the other one said, "I see your heiny, so black and shiny, it makes me giggle to see it wiggle." On and on it went with "einy, meiny, miney mo, catch a (n-word) by his toe, if he hollers, let him go, einy, meiny, miney mo." Of course, they found my embarrassment to be entertaining. As children often do, they took it a little too far until I cried.

I wish I had known then that not reacting to this particular type of teasing would have ended it more quickly. As a matter of fact, I wish I could pass that lesson on to my own children. I've tried with no success.

It seems to me there are certain lessons that have to be experienced. Its like there's an invisible force field around children's brains that won't let verbal knowledge resonate until they've personally endured and experienced teasing for themselves. Maybe a brilliant God designed it this way so we learn endurance and build character. My siblings had fun teasing and embarrassing me. I probably enjoyed the attention but something in my stomach hurt for Rosie and it was something I didn't understand.

I contacted Roosevelt recently to ask him if I could use his real name in my story. I have changed most of the other character's names to protect their privacy and respect any discrepancies in my truth. However, it was important to me to use Roosevelt's real name if possible because I wanted to acknowledge the enduring love I felt for my sweet precious little friend. When I think of telling the truth, I ask myself if it is good and if it is absolutely true. If it is, I feel good about saying it and if it isn't, I try to let it go. I find it easy to tell the truth but to always say good things, especially when I'm hurt is more of a challenge.

This particular motto is inspired by the bible verse Philippians 4:8 which reads

Finally, brethren, whatever is true, whatever is honorable, whatever is right, whatever is pure, whatever is lovely, whatever is of good repute, if there is any excellence and if anything worthy of praise, dwell on these things.

Rosie said, "I'm so proud of you for doing this, (writing this book). We need more people to stand up to prejudice and I'm glad you're taking the initiative to do so." I also asked Roosevelt "Rosie" how he felt about me using the word "black" instead of "African American." He said exactly this "To me, the term 'black' is acceptable. I don't like to use African American but that's just my choice. Either one is fine but if you want to avoid possible backlash or harsh critics you should use AA. Actually, you should use both. All you have to do is clarify why you choose to use the former term and why now you choose the latter." He nailed it. That was exactly what I wanted and need to do.

I currently live in Washington DC where being politically correct is critical to survival. However, when I talk about the past in Panama City, Florida, it feels disingenuous to say, "African American" because we had never heard of or used that term back then.

When I refer to someone as being "black" in this book, I know that I am remembering a different time. I'm referring to a place and/or time where one could easily get away with wearing a KKK Halloween costume or painting their face black to portray a black person. Recently, in 2019, Ralph Northam, a Democratic governor was tainted by a photo where he had decades before dressed up as either a KKK member or had a painted face (I believe it was never determined as to which one it was.) He apologized for the hurt that his decision had caused then and now. How can I explain my understanding of what he is saying? So many people find it abhorrent but do they understand just how ignorant and insensitive toward racism we were conditioned to be? I've tried time and time again to find the words to explain it. I just don't think those words exist but those of us who experienced and ignorantly participated understand. Inherent prejudice comes from ignorance. I don't intend the word ignorance to be an insult to anyone and I own that I swam in that very pool myself.

This is how I feel about ignorance. We are all ignorant about things we don't understand. I love making random analogies and you might find this one way out there, but here it goes. The first time I went to a sushi restaurant, I was ignorant about sushi. Of course, I knew sushi was raw fish and rice all wrapped up in a roll. I knew it was to be eaten with soy sauce and chopsticks. Not until I sat down in the restaurant and confessed to my date and our server that I was a sushi neophyte did I learn how to order sushi and how to appreciate it. I had to realize it, admit it, and choose to do something about it before I could understand and embrace eating sushi.

A completely unrelated example even though it also involves food: I ate meat for the first two decades of my life and never once consciously acknowledged I was eating an animal that had been hurt and killed. A hamburger was just a hamburger, not a grated up, formerly living being. Of course, I knew subconsciously I was eating dead animals all those years but it wasn't until I stopped and truly thought about it that I made a conscious decision to stop. Now, when I see an image of a happy little pig on the sign at a barbecue restaurant, I find it odd. I don't think the pigs would be remotely happy to know they were going to be made into bacon! There's nothing cute about slaughtering pigs, chickens or cows yet we advertise with happy caricatures of the very animals we eat. I notice these things because I'm no longer ignorant to what it actually is and how it affects others (In this case, 'others' being animals.) I also realize that it's my personal choice to be a vegetarian and that most people are not. I'm also not saying carnivores are ignorant. I'm just confessing that I was ignorant in this case and the sushi case as examples.

I feel the same way about all kinds of prejudice. Maybe, just maybe if many prejudiced people knew that their prejudiced and racist jokes, ideas, and actions were hurting other souls, maybe they would have done things differently. Maybe I'm even guilty. Maybe because of my upbringing, I have done things that have made someone of another race feel bad unknowingly due to ignorance. I may never know.

The incident with my siblings regarding Rosie was my first conscious introduction to prejudice and racism. I don't think it ever occurred to my brothers and sisters that their jokes were hurtful. As a matter of fact, I'm absolutely positive they didn't.

It was Jade who told me that African Americans try to have as many children as they can so that eventually, they can take over the world. It was Jade who told me that African Americans have an extra muscle in their legs. It wasn't until I was a young adult that it occurred to me that human beings are all made up of the same exact stuff and that race is just a social construct. Are both my parents to blame for this or is inherent prejudice passed down from the ages? I blame those unanswered questions; the ones Jade refused to answer and the ones I was too afraid to ask. Regardless, prejudice began to creep into my life and just like one little mouse enters a home undetected, before long it became an infestation.

In first grade, I asked Jade, "Why are white people better than black people? God could have put my soul in a black body instead of a white one." She chuckled in sneering merriment, "That's a crazy thought. There's no way you could have been black when both of your parents are white." She continued to snicker to herself as she shooed me away like a fly.

My dad was born in Athens, Alabama and lived across the street from a cotton field. Most of the cotton pickers were black and as a child I often heard black people referred to as "cotton pickers."

It could have been many decades before his time or something he saw as a little boy but I remember him telling a story about a black man being lynched and dragged through the town from the back of a car. I tried to find this story online but apparently there were thousands of reported lynchings during that time and no knows how many went unreported, especially in small towns. Jade was originally from Mississippi. According to the NAACP, Mississippi had even more reported lynchings than Alabama. My point? This is what white people did to black people in the small towns where my parental influences grew up.

It's been over thirty years since I've lived down south. My accent is still thick enough to elicit questions about where in the South I'm from. I proudly own my southern heritage and I find joy, fondness and pride in so many southern ways. However, having been estranged from the South, I've become a fair observer of a stereotypical mindset and an inherent prejudice that I can no longer deny.

I spent a great deal of my childhood cheerleading. It was everything to me and Homecoming was always the highlight of the season. It was tradition to issue the cheerleaders huge white mum corsages. Each had a googly eyed little bumble bee made out of pipe cleaner. Each corsage had a big orange bow to match our cheerleading uniforms. We paraded across the field with our escorts and lined up in a row. The previous year's homecoming queen walked back and forth behind us until she stopped behind whoever was going to be the new homecoming queen and crowned her head.

I don't remember if this particular incident was in the fourth or fifth grade but it was time for the twelve cheerleaders to choose our escorts at the last practice before Homecoming. We each took a number out of a hat.

The coaches lined up the 13 first string players for us to choose our escorts. It wasn't my lucky day because I drew number 12 and was left with only two boys to choose from. One just so happened to be black and the best player on the team. The other choice was Tommy who was a cute little "redhead" with a face full of freckles. I loved both boys as childhood friends I had known since kindergarten. I clearly remember standing there with something like the Jeopardy music playing in my head and I was thinking, "Keith (the black boy) is our best player and my friend" I didn't consciously think that I didn't "want" him to be my escort because he was black but in hindsight, subconsciously, I knew that I wasn't supposed to choose Keith.

There was complete silence when I announced that I wanted "the black boy," Keith as my escort. Jade was overtly cold and quiet on the drive home as if I had done something unspeakably wrong. She was also clearly uncomfortable and embarrassed at the homecoming game. Keith grinned proudly as he escorted me across the field.

Even though I had been growing up with racism, I was still too young and naïve to understand exactly what I had done "wrong." I didn't inherently understand the unspoken social strata of the South and this in and of itself was a disappointment to Jade. Many years later, I saw Keith's mother at the Piggly Wiggly grocery store. She raved about my homecoming choice and how much it meant to her and to Keith. This moment was another invaluable stepping stone in the discovery that I was capable of making good, right and wise decisions on my own.

I suddenly had no doubt that I had actually done something very right despite Jade. When I look back on it, I believe it may have been one of the bravest choices I ever made. For that brief moment I didn't care what Jade thought.

I was beginning to see that Jade wasn't necessarily perfect or right. I started watching her more discerningly. This was my first inkling that I could secretly have my own opinions. I just couldn't express them. Not yet.

CHAPTER 5-CHURCH IS NOT THE PROBLEM

Nothing was more important than church in my family, at least that's how I saw it. We attended service three times a week unless someone was really sick. We took everything that was written in the Bible literally and there was no tolerance for any variation in understanding. I wanted to believe everything we were told with all my heart and I tried. I even prayed that God would give me more faith and take my doubts away. Coincidentally, I still do.

Although I was given an explanation for many of our beliefs, I still didn't understand why we couldn't have a piano in our church building, why everyone except the people who went to our church were going to hell or why it was frowned upon to go to the prom.

So many things didn't make sense to me intellectually and I felt like I was a prisoner of the fraudulent role I was assigned to play. The more I studied the bible, the more questions I had and the more I doubted its literal meaning. How could a loving God that's omnipotent, omnipresent and all loving allow parents to beat us leaving bruises and welts on our tiny bodies? Why did Jade pinch and twist the skin on my arms in the church service whenever I popped the joints of my fingers, didn't sing the hymns or stopped paying attention? Would God want her to do that to me right there in the house of The Lord? Would he want her to tell James and me that we were worthless, failures, ugly? Wasn't it a birthright to be loved by our parents? I grew up in a perpetual state of confusion and fear of God coming out of the clouds and taking me to hell at any moment. I felt guilty for how I felt about Jesus. I thought, "If God's not a person, how can he know what its like to be a human father?" There was always an answer in the sermons. "Because he's omniscient, of course." How could he be all knowing and all powerful and still allow bad things to happen to people? "If I was omnipotent, I wouldn't let people and animals get hurt," I thought.

I recently heard a preacher on the radio talking about the Himalayan Mountains. He said that 50% of their children die before their eighth birthday and the rest of the people live in a hellish poverty, never hear of God and therefore, they are condemned to spend hell on Earth and for eternity. Why would this God we praise and sing songs of love and compassion be so unfair? I wanted to know these things; I wanted to talk about it. I still wonder how much stronger my faith could have been if Jade would have just allowed me to ask. Even as a little child, I couldn't help but think if I believed dying on the cross would save all of mankind from burning up in hell for eternity, I'd hammer the nail into my own hands. I wondered, "Who wouldn't?" I thought, "Maybe Jesus believed he was the son of God with all his heart, but maybe he was mistaken." We would jump in front of a bullet for our children, wouldn't anyone do the same? I had a problem with Jesus for this reason. I loved him and in my twenties when I eventually "fell away" I missed him. I was out on the dance floor losing my religion and feeling really guilty at the same time. I wanted to understand what I was told to believe yet every time I asked Jade to help me understand she refused.

As a young adult, I tried to find these answers myself through religious courses, books, talking to people of other faiths and I have come and am still coming to my own beliefs. I just can't help but long for the kind of faith that sets in with an open dialogue during those formative years. I believe it would have been easier for my brothers, sisters and me.

Growing up, in our church, we were expected at around the age of thirteen to come forward during the invitation song, announce that Jesus is the son of God and then be dunked in a giant tub with the entire congregation watching. I wasn't going to do this for various reasons. I couldn't imagine walking down the center aisle with over 100 people staring at my buck teeth and yellow eyes. I didn't want to have my name announced out loud and to be dunked under water in front of anyone. I was absolutely terrified to do it. In some ways I wanted to do it just to please my family and just in case God did come down from the clouds; he might suck me up to heaven in a clear tube. (That's how I imagined it anyway.)
I just couldn't bring myself to walk down that aisle. Instead I kept my head down in my hymnal every service until the invitation song was finally over.

I endured years of guilt trips from my parents and Demi. At about my twelfth birthday, Demi began to nudge me and kick me during the invitation song. I sometimes felt the preacher (my dad's best friend) was speaking directly to me during the sermon. I began hating going to church. The more I started to think for myself, the more church felt somber and ascetic. Although the atmosphere at times felt a little quixotic, I don't have anything but appreciation and residual love for the people at church. This is why. It was Jade who enforced the beliefs of our church on me in a way that seemed to suck so much joy out of being a human being. It was Jade who I went to with my questions and Jade who shot me down and told me not to think for myself. It was Jade who had driven a wedge between my dad and me and Jade who I grew to fear more and more each day. Church was not the problem.

I wondered why the Davenports were the only black family that occasionally came to church. They were a large and lovely family. The Davenports were treated with the kindest of southern hospitality. I noticed Jade's voice sounded higher when she spoke to them in the same way she might speak to a pet or a little child.

They were never included in some conversations and fellowship the way they should have been. They eventually stopped coming and I wondered if there might be a black heaven separate from the white heaven and if they had finally realized they'd been knocking on the wrong door. I fantasized about going to their house and telling them I was sorry from all of us. I wanted them to come back but to come back welcomed and I knew that I couldn't make that happen, not back then.

Summer bible school was a different story. My dad drove our pastel yellow "J.O.Y." bus into the subsidized housing neighborhood picking up all races of children for vacation bible school. JOY stood for "Jesus, Others, and then, Yourself," and was painted on both sides of the bus. It was lovely. I loved riding with him and sharing my church and my God with everyone. It felt right for me to be inclusive and I didn't feel a difference between us. We never recruited these children's families to come to church and the children seldom came back after their one week of bible school. I suppose we were checking off that box of going into the world and sharing the gospel.

This mindset can't be blamed on Jade or the church. You see, we were just ignorant to the inherent prejudice we were born into and each of us has individually either evolved or we haven't. I like to believe the vast majority has evolved far beyond this antiquated attitude. I think some people want to deny it ever happened or that we were a part of it, but we were. I believe we have to hold it in our hands, look at it and acknowledge it before we can truly set it free. I think it needs to be said out loud, no matter how uncomfortable it is.

CHAPTER 6-WHAT'S A PICKANNY

Pickaninny (also picaninny, piccaninny or pickaninny) is a North American historical racial slur which refers to a dark- skinned child of African descent. -Wikipedia

When my dad married Jade, we had two quilts someone on his side of the family had made. They were covered with figures of people wearing overalls and had black faces. I loved our quilts. They were just "our quilts." We had an adorable little mutt named Charlie Brown from before our melding with the Jade package. Although Jade's poodle slept in bed with her, Charlie Brown was assigned to sleep in the laundry room. She put down our quilts for Charlie Brown. She called them our "Pickaninny" quilts. I never once questioned what a "pickaninny" was and just assumed it was the proper name for a quilt. Years later, Jade opened a country store where she sold wooden knick-knacks and household decor with a country flare. She had various dolls and figurines with black faces and she called them "pickaninnies." She had probably been raised to call them "pickaninnies". How were we to know this wasn't what they were called? We were just children.

In ninth grade, I waited for Jade to pick me up from school. The only other student waiting was a black boy and we were chatting and laughing while we waited for our rides. When I happily jumped in the back seat of Jades car (I was never allowed to ride in the front), I was startled to see she was furious. She told me not to ever let her catch me talking to a black boy again. She told me "Only white trash girls talk to black boys." These were strong words for a fourteen-year-old girl to hear from her only female role model. I never wanted to be mistaken for trash and was striving daily and desperately to be ladylike and respectable. I was trying so hard to be like Jade so I could win her approval and love. I made sure this never happened again.

Occasionally, we saw a black man with a white woman at a restaurant or as in a particular memory on the back of a motorcycle. Jade never failed to point out the woman must be white trash. She would say the white girl couldn't get a white boyfriend so she had to settle for a black one. She would talk about how black men think that it's a status symbol to have a white girlfriend. I wondered why "white trash" and "black" were equal in her mind because I couldn't see that. I didn't know that I was allowed to disagree in my heart and in my mind. As Jade's "daughter," I actually wasn't allowed to disagree about anything.

For years to come, I would wonder how we could control who we fell in love with but that question was fleeting in my mind. This is why. If a respectable white girl didn't associate herself with black boys, there would be no chance of that happening; that was the rule. I am embarrassed to confess that when I saw interracial couples as a teenager and young adult, I felt sorry for them in a way. Recently, while watching the movie "Bohemian Rhapsody" a particular scene resonated with me because it reminded me of how I felt many years ago. Freddie Mercury nervously told his wife, Mary Austin he thought he might be bi-sexual. She replied that she already knew this and that he was indeed actually gay. She told him she loved and accepted him but said sadly, "You're going to have a hard life." I thought back about the prejudice we were taught to feel toward anyone remotely ethnic and without doubt anyone who dared to be gay. Jade told me that homosexuality was beyond a sin; it was a mental disorder. I believed her. I pitied anyone who wasn't fortunate enough to be white and I pitied anyone who wasn't heterosexual in the same way I pitied anyone with a physical deformity or a homeless person. I wondered why this spectacular God we sang praises to on Sundays would allow such things to happen.

"These things" being deformities, the "mental illness" of being gay and the "unfortunate" state of being ethnic.

In hindsight, it even seemed normal to me that most of the black children in our school sat at the same lunch table in the corner of the room away from the white children.
It wasn't until my twenty-year high school reunion that I noticed. Just like the lunchroom twenty years prior, the African Americans seemed to be gathered at one table. At the reunion, it was the same in that way but it was still different, evolved. It no longer felt like a divide. They were no longer sitting together because of backward southern social bias. They were sitting with the people they had been friends with in high school and with whom they had kept in touch with throughout the years. We were all happy to see each other and everyone intermingled. Twenty years and the freedom to love who we want had changed us and brought us back together the way we should have always been.

After high school, I went to college in Tuscaloosa, Alabama. My boyfriend belonged to a prestigious fraternity and lived in a big antebellum house with a pack of privileged white boys. All of the houses on fraternity row looked relatively the same. Behind fraternity row was a dirt road with run-down houses. These were the black fraternity houses and I often heard it referred to as "Nig Row." To hear this made me cringe, broke my heart and seemed so very wrong.

I remember one particular boy from Montgomery, Alabama would often refer to certain African Americans as "first generation uprights." Finally, I asked what he meant. He looked at me as if I should have known and said that it was a joke regarding evolution and that they looked more like apes than people. I wondered how he could think this was funny. This was 30 years ago.

Recently, I reached out to white and black friends from my childhood to make sure my memories were accurate. I was happy to learn that most of them had evolved with me in enlightened and inspiring ways.

I found this on an old friend's Facebook page and it confirms the racism I observed.
"I wonder if Lynn Haven was impacted by redlining. I can recall all of the roads were paved except between 14th and 17th streets between Pennsylvania and Mississippi Avenues. Most if not all the residents were of African American descent."

We didn't understand the mechanics of redlining and systemic racism growing up but we felt it and I knew subconsciously it was happening.

In the United States and Canada, Redlining is the systematic denial of various services to residents of specific, often racially associated, neighborhoods or communities, either directly or through the selective raising of prices.- *Wikipedia*

I interviewed the only hispanic person I remembered from high school. He told me that he suffered prejudice from both the caucasians and the African Americans. He said he felt completely isolated until he eventually joined the football team which was the only place he felt a part of anything at all. He said that felt we didn't even know that he existed until he joined the football team but I remember him before that and don't remember purposely excluding him anymore than any of the other boys. However, I do remember in fifth grade, Denise George would put her jacket on backwards to imitate a priest and perform marriage ceremonies between the white girls and the white boys. I married lots of boys that year, but none of them were black or hispanic. I wonder what they were doing while we were getting married. Were they watching from afar or were they off doing their own thing without a care? I don't know.

My life took me further away from the deep south, to Atlanta and then eventually I landed in Dallas where I spent most of my twenties. I taught aerobics at a very high-end gym where I met a lot of nice, accomplished young men. I never considered dating members for the same and obvious reasons why anyone wouldn't want to date customers where they work. However, an extremely handsome, refined, and tenacious young black man from the gym began creatively pursuing me for quite some time. I wouldn't consider dating him in the same way that I wouldn't consider learning to speak French and visiting the south of France. Neither was heard of where I came from. I had never fathomed international travel in the same way I had never considered the truth that I actually "could" date a black man. It was inconceivable.

After completely charming me day after day, I finally agree to go out with this gentleman. Instead of flowers or like many dates who brought me nothing at all, he presented me with the book "The Notebook." Little did I know it was a best seller and would later become a movie because I didn't have time to read. But in hindsight, what a tasteful gesture. We went out for a lovely meal but I was terribly uncomfortable. I felt eyes all around judging me and in my mind calling me "white trash." I couldn't wait for him to take me home.

We had a glass of wine on my balcony and I dropped my glass in the shrubs below. He offered to go and get it for me but I said that I thought it was time for him to go. The next morning, I found the wine glass sitting by my front door. I thought of him searching for my wine glass in the prickly bushes below my balcony and thought it was incredibly sweet and adorable. I don't remember exactly what happened after that but I never saw him again by choice. I can bet that he went on to marry some beautiful, accomplished woman that deserved someone like him and I'm guessing that he never thought of me again. I'd love to apologize to him for caring what strangers in the restaurant thought and for not giving him a chance regardless of whether or not he remembers or cares. I can't do this because I don't even remember his name.

I'm so grateful to have escaped the inherent prejudice that was forced on me as a child. I don't even think about what color someone's skin is anymore, and ironically I've also learned a little French and traveled to the south of France. I never thought I would do that either

THE GIFT OF JADE-CHAPTER 7

In Chinese culture, Jade symbolizes the five virtues of humanity; Courage, Compassion, Modesty, Justice and Wisdom. It is believed to bring good luck, friendship, peace and harmony. If only we had been Chinese.

When Jade entered our lives and I was about to turn five years old, my new sister Demi and my original sister Kristen were both teenagers and moved into a big room in the front of the house. My new brother, Max and my original brother James shared a room even though there was about an eight year age difference between them. This didn't last long and James eventually moved into my room so Max could have his own room. In the meantime, I was issued my own room next to Jade and my dad's room. This was probably because I was painfully afraid of the dark or maybe just because I was the youngest.

It's funny to me now because my brothers and sisters occasionally went outside to my window and whispered creepy things or howled. Then, they would scratch on my window with tree branches and wait for me to scream. I was so incredibly petrified, I would lay there trying with all my might to jump out of bed and go get my dad but time after time, I couldn't move. It was relatively innocent teasing on their part but I don't think they ever understood how scared I really was at the time and just how funny I think it is now. It would be fun to reminisce with them, but I just can't. This is a normal childhood memory just like other people have and I like having that. I also loved that Jade decorated my bedroom with girly things and introduced me to new characters like Holly Hobby and Raggedy Ann. I had every reason to think we would all live happily ever after.

Our new family had new rules. So many rules. We were not allowed to enter our parents' bedroom without permission as if there were an invisible line drawn across the doorway. It was hard to break the habit of crawling into bed and snuggling with my dad. I remembered that before Jade came along, James, Kristen and I all three climbed into bed with our dad and snuggled like kittens. I missed those days so much.

I missed snuggling with him on the carpet of our old house while he fell asleep watching football. I missed talking to him while he tried to watch football and asking him questions about woodpeckers. I missed watching "The Jeffersons" and "Sanford and Son" with him on the floor in front of our couch when it was just the four of us. Instead, he now watched it in his room with Jade or by himself because we weren't allowed in there. I could hear him laughing down the hall though, and that made me happy and became the new normal. My dad was just perfect until he married Jade. Although, I now realize our life was just fine before Jade, we had every reason to believe we now had more, a new, beautiful mom and an extra brother and sister. I thought our lives were going to be better than ever before.

My new teenage sister, Demi played with me sometimes. Any time she would give me any attention at all thrilled me; in the beginning, I thought of her the way little girls think of a princess. She was tiny with long, stringy brown hair and I thought she was just fascinating. She had taken ballet and tap and played the piano, things that would only be in my dreams.

The five of us had some really good times together too. We have fantastic memories where we pretended my new teenage brother Max was Bob Barker. My sisters played the pretty models from The Price is Right while my brother James and I played contestants and guessed the prices of canned vegetables and jars of jelly. Max had an amplifier and a microphone that he used to run the show. We took a little yellow plastic Volkswagen car and placed it on a record player turntable. We turned the speed down so low that the car would spin around slowly on display as the grand prize just like the real cars on the show.

We each had our own fishing poles and fished off the canal in the backyard with hot dogs and bologna. We caught croaker and pulled up several crabs at a time. I laughed at the crabs as they all clung desperately to the pieces of hot dog dangling from the line. We set them loose in the grass and watched them click their claws and waddle sideways until they eventually plunged off the sea wall and back into the water. Sometimes, we turned them over and rubbed their bellies until they fell asleep. Once a lady across the canal caught a pregnant stingray. We all gazed in amazement as baby stingrays emerged from the mother stingray, slid off the seawall and swam away. These are the memories we talked about at holidays years later when we were still a family.

When I think of these good memories, I find it hard to believe that my brothers and sisters are so estranged. None of them will speak to me. Kristen won't speak to Demi. James will only speak to Kristen and Max. Max is rather diplomatic and speaks to everyone except for me. Demi would probably speak to any of us but we'd have to push ourselves on her and even then she would keep her distance. I tried for many years and I always walked away hurt. Demi would probably appease us if we reached out to her, but nothing substantial would come of it. Not only would Jade not approve but those days are just gone.

Gas-lighting is a form of psychological manipulation that seeks to sow seeds of doubt in a targeted individual or in members of a targeted group, making them question their own memory, perception, and sanity.
Wikipedia

Jade successfully drove wedges between us and discredited me so that no one would believe what she's done to me. I can explain exactly how and why she spun her web and how she captured and sucked the blood out of each of us. If no one in the family trusts me and if everyone thinks I'm malevolent, then nothing I tell them about her will matter. She is determined to keep it that way.

I loved it when all seven of us piled into our big blue Buick to go to the beach. Sometimes, my siblings would put me on the floorboard underneath their legs or toss me up into that little platform between the back seat and the back window.

My siblings and I swam out to the sandbar where we could stand and filled up our buckets with sand dollars which we would later take home to bleach. Jade sat under an umbrella with a hat and read. She didn't interact with us but she looked pretty with her perfectly piled up hair, her Jackie O sunglasses and her long legs glistening in the sun.

Jade wouldn't allow sand in her car so my dad would twist up a towel and whip it off of us the way frat boys twist their towels to snap each other. I hated this part. It always seemed to put a damper on a lovely day as it felt like we were being punished. Our new siblings, Demi and Max never had to have sand snapped off of their legs as I recall. I assumed they were less sandy than the rest of us. I also began to understand they were superior and I didn't question the normalcy or the fairness in it. It was just a new normal and it was never spoken of.

All five of us worked together to make our Halloween decorations the best and scariest in the neighborhood. We gathered moss from trees and made gravestones that said R.I.P. We played scary music and made Halloween an absolute blast for several years.

When the first Christmas at our new house came, I thought I had died and gone to heaven. My stash was full of dolls, a doll house, a new bike, a tea set, a miniature table and chairs. It was a miracle to me. This new life was so fantastic that I didn't mind the new rules and hardly noticed that my dad stopped hugging me or showing me affection.

I didn't know what "I-injoidit" meant but I knew I had to eat everything on my plate, ask to be excused and say, "I-injoidit" before I could leave the table. I thought maybe it was a fancy French word. It was never explained to me that I was telling Jade I enjoyed her meal. I can see now how they would have assumed I understood what those simple words meant but instead I was just trying to do exactly what I was told without question.

When she wasn't at work or reading a book in her room, Jade was usually stationed in the kitchen preparing the meals we always ate as a family. She was a fantastic cook and baked beautiful and delicious pies and cakes for birthdays and holidays. Even in gourmet bakeries and five star restaurants I have never had better desserts. She made pot roast, fried pork chops, salmon croquettes or lasagna. There was always a starch liked canned peas, beans or fried okra. I didn't like certain things like canned beans or ham but I had to eat them and pretend to enjoy them. If I didn't, I would get a whipping, of course. Fortunately, I was never forced to eat the fried okra because other family members loved it and there never seemed to be enough. Demi told me secretly that okra was really fried grasshoppers and I was so relieved to see the empty grease soaked plate once it was gone. We never had salad. We never had fresh broccoli, asparagus or zucchini. I didn't know what an artichoke or an avocado was until I was an adult. Not eating Jade's food was considered insulting to her and was often followed by a lecture about the starving children in Ethiopia. I never understood how me not eating my food helped the Ethiopian children. The concept was never explained to me but I remember thinking that there were many, many meals I would have been happy to give those Ethiopian children if they weren't so darn far away.

We were terrified of whippings but somehow couldn't seem to avoid them. I don't remember getting whippings before Jade came along. I guess you could say, "Once the honeymoon wore off" we received whippings regularly. Down south in the 70's, whipping were just as common as not wearing seat belts and having a dog off a leash. They all happened without a second thought and are all three illegal now.

In the beginning, Jade had swooped in with gifts, new siblings and a trip to Disney World. I was so excited to see this Dumbo with big ears like mine that she had told me about. Our trip to Disney World with our new siblings and our new mom was completely magical for me, just like the wide eyed children you see in commercials today. I suppose it is magical for all children. The memory can be great on some days. On other days it reminds me of the way human traffickers entice children with soft drinks to later exploit them. In hindsight, it almost feels that Jade was baiting us just to later suffocate our spirits and cut out our hearts.

Jade had caught my dad hook, line and sinker. To him, her word was gold and whatever she wanted him to do, he did. Soon after we all settled in, our new family seemed to shift from something fun and new to a regimen of structure; expectations were high and consequences were harsh. Jade wrote the rule book and she wanted us trained to be more like Demi and Max. We were like feral cats to her and she was going to tame us. We learned how to hold our forks, speak proper grammar, brush our teeth, and how to sit and stand.

I was tenacious to please and seemed to meet her expectations much easier than James and Kristen. I just couldn't stop sucking my thumb and strands of my newly grown long hair. I had never had long hair before and I couldn't stop putting strands of it in my mouth. She put a pacifier on a ribbon around my neck and required me to wear it in public. I was forced to publicly suck on it if I ever dared to put a finger or a string of hair in my mouth. I remembered being incredibly embarrassed yet I guess her method worked. I eventually stopped putting my thumb in my mouth but the shame I felt lingered.

When the Jade package was still shiny and new, she was preparing to host a Tupperware party at our new home. Chickenpox was going around at school and the very morning of her party, I developed a fever and rash that she knew was the beginning of chickenpox. She chose a long sleeved blouse for me to wear and handed me some pink Bayer baby aspirin which I thought were delicious. She told me not to scratch and not to tell anyone about the rash. I went to first grade with her instructions playing over and over in my head. The first thing the teachers did was an inspection to see if any of us had chickenpox and Jade was called to pick me up. On the drive home, she told me that I had ruined her tupperware party.

She ran a bath for me and told me to stay in the tub until her guests had all gone. It seemed as if the party continued into perpetuity and I became incredibly bored and hungry. I don't know why but I decided to eat the white bar of Dial soap as I had run out of other things to do. I immediately started hiccuping and bubbles came out of my mouth. This lead to throwing up which alerted Jade and she came in to find out what I had done. In hindsight, I find it hysterical but at the time she didn't laugh. She rarely laughed at all.

We all went to see the movie "Song of the South." I think because it was my first movie, it remained my favorite children's movie for decades to come. I never had any idea the movie would be labeled racist and put away in Disney's vault in 1986. In 2010, the movie would later be called "antiquated" and "fairly offensive" by Disney's own CEO. It never occurred to any of us the movie was racist, probably because we were inherently prejudiced. We just didn't know it. It felt like I was floating on a cloud of happiness as we left the theatre. In the parking lot, Jade looked down and gasped at my wet pants. I had been so engrossed in the movie my Sprite spilled in my lap without my slightest notice. She insisted I had wet my pants and made me walk in front and away from everyone else on the way back to the car. She decided humiliation was the way to train the runt of this feral litter.

My brother James seemed to have the most trouble measuring up to Jade's expectations. I don't know why because he was adorable and funny. He was a cute little mischievous boy with blue eyes like my dad's and cowlicks in the temples of his brown hair. He tried but he just couldn't seem to do anything right. When my dad came home from a hard days work selling hearing aids, Jade would wait at the front door to tell him what James had done wrong. My dad would drag James by the underarm into his room and beat him with his big leather belt. He would growl "stop crying or I'm going to give you something to cry about." I don't know if he stopped the whipping once we were able to taper our cries to a whimper or until he had worked out his own frustration. Right or wrong, my dad believed wholeheartedly in "spare the rod, spoil the child" and I remember him afterwards sometimes say, "It hurts me more than it hurts you."

In one of my recently recovered journals from the 90's I wrote verbatim "I went from adoring my brother James to cringing if he accidentally brushed up against me in our crowded car." I started thinking there was something gross about him. People often assure me that its common to go through a phase where you believe your brother has cooties. I understand that and believe there is some common truth it in. However, there was more. I continued in this journal, "But I knew I was expected by Jade to hate him. If I wanted to be loved by my new mom, I knew that I must reject James." As long as I behaved, I was quiet, made good grades and didn't ask for anything; if I did everything just the way that Jade expected, then I would maybe win her acceptance. If I did these things to her approval, I believed I would earn her love. In hindsight, it was a temporary tolerance I was granted, not love. She never said she loved me. Maybe she did love me down deep inside and in a way I can't understand. I don't think it's completely fair to say how another person felt. I just wanted to believe she loved me, so I did. More than twenty years ago, I continued to write in my journal, "If Jade caught me playing with James or spending time with Kristen, she would shoot me with darts from her eyes. As if I had just received an electrical shock, I would immediately cease contact. I would then try to redeem myself by helping Jade with a chore or by spending time with Demi if she happened to be in the mood to placate me."

I was so relieved to see what I wrote in this very old journal was verbatim/consistent with what I remember today. I continued "Jade took me along with her to many places when I was small. I guess she had to legally, but I liked to think she enjoyed my company." Many of these memories are pleasant enough. I treasured time with her and it seems that it didn't matter to her then and it doesn't matter to her now.

She took me along to collect some monkey grass from someone who had extra growing in their yard. We pulled out unnoticeable little clumps and then took them home and dotted our driveway with it. Eventually it grew into plush solid rows as a frame to our yard and I thought it was beautiful. Most of all, it was something I thought, "My mom" and I had created together. Through the years, whenever someone mentioned how nice our monkey grass looked, Jade always took credit for it and told the story as if I hadn't been there. Coincidentally, I didn't consciously notice that until now that I think back on it. I also remember that as we were going to get the monkey grass, an elderly man was walking down the road when Jade stopped to ask him a directional question. He was extremely discombobulated and couldn't answer and didn't seem to know who or where he was. As we drove away she mumbled "Alzheimer's" but I thought I heard "Old Timers." For many years, I thought Alzheimers was "Old Timers" and I also wondered why she didn't try to help him find his way home and I worried myself sick about him. Many times over the years I have heard stories on the news about a missing elderly person or something to do with Alzheimers and I think back to that day we did nothing. I also think about how Jade was always doing good things for other people on display; when she could get recognition yet other times, when no one was watching, it seemed to me that she turned the other way. She didn't talk to me much but I was allowed to be in her presence and with her perpetual silence. If I tried to talk to her, she would shut me down with "Don't be a Chatty Kathy," or "Do you EVER shut up?"

Her radio never changed from a 70's easy listening station and I learned the words to every song they played. I looked out the window and pictured the stories behind the songs in the same way you visualize a story when you read a book. I particularly remember the song "Brandy" by Looking Glass. I painted the most romantic movie in my mind about a server in a harbor town who loved a sailor who brought her exotic gifts from far away places. He loved her but he just couldn't lure himself away from the sea. I loved "Raindrops keep falling on my Head" by BJ Thomas and "Tie A Yellow Ribbon" by Tony Orlando and Dawn. I still love 70's easy listening songs. Most of them bring back fond memories and will always be a part of my life. My husband and children laugh at me now because I know every word to almost every 70's easy listening and love song. They don't always remind me of Jade and I sing and hum them happily. However, sometimes they do remind me of her and I can't do anything about that. "They" say (whoever "They" are) sometimes you have to sever a relationship and I know that it's true. Remembering these songs fondly begs the question "Was Jade all bad?" It does cause circular reasoning but my answer is "No! Without question. No one is." Yet for years, I felt extreme guilt for letting her go. I made the conscious decision to sever the relationship but yet had some good memories too. She fixed my rotten teeth, my pigeon toes and let me help her weed the garden but she tortured me emotionally and psychologically. Once I finally chose to cut her out of my life, her birthday and Mother's Day would roll around and guilt me. Even after we were estranged, one Mother's Day, I wrote her a letter listing the good memories and nice things she had done for me. I didn't mention any of the bad. At that point, I needed to acknowledge her for the things she had genuinely done for me. Looking back now, I no longer have that need. I have already acknowledged her for all the good things she had done for me on Mother's Day.

She has yet to acknowledge the mental abuse or to try and help me mend relationships she has sabotaged for me. I no longer feel indebted to her.

Coincidentally, I credit Oprah Winfrey for giving me the courage to sever my relationship with Jade. It wasn't one quote or one show or one article. It was an accumulation of her good advice that came to me and whispered "let her go." It was when I had a toddler and a baby of my own and it said, "Kathryn, its time to let go. You must take care of yourself so that you can take care of these little boys. Don't expose them to this toxic relationship. Oprah approves." Don't worry. I wasn't hearing Oprah's voice in my head. It was finally time to let go and words of her wisdom gave me comfort, that's all.

I wrote Jade a letter telling her I was setting her free of me. I explained that I felt I was pushing myself on her. I wrote this from a hospital in South Africa where I was alone having a major surgery. Circumstances required me to be alone; my husband and two small children remained in Mozambique. I think it was the sense of being alone that reminded me I really didn't have a mom.

It was a time when I felt a very deep and painful absence. She retorted with a nasty letter telling me she would keep it with all the other hostile letters I've written her over the years. I read it just before I called a cab to pick me up from the B&B where I was recovering. I sat in the cab and quietly sobbed. The cab driver said. "You are in MOURNING and I can feel your grief." I WAS in mourning of the relationship I had wanted so badly but never had to begin with.

My heart's desire is not to demonize Jade or say my entire childhood was tragic. If it was, I wouldn't have included some of those 70's songs in the lullabies I sang to both of my own babies decades later. I still love easy listening songs from the 70's and there is an association with Jade, not entirely though. There are also my private moments alone with my imagination. Just because I was in her car, they were still somehow my own personal memories of me with "my" songs. That's how I really feel. Yes, Jade is in there residually, but not enough to flatten my soufflé.

Strangely, there are things I despise because they remind me of Jade. I don't even consciously think of her when I see them yet I can hardly bear the colors burgundy and forest green. There was a time when our brick house on the canal was heavily ornamented with these colors. These colors surrounded me during a time when Jade was particularly cruel to me and I just can't stand these colors. I also hate holly bushes, which we had growing in front of our house on Driftwood Drive. The house I live in with my husband now has a holly bush on the corner and I want it chopped down. My husband thinks it's silly of me but I just hate it. I hate it like Jenny hated her childhood home in the movie "Forrest Gump." I thought it was a beautiful gesture when Forrest had the house demolished in honor of her even after her death. I think the least my husband can do is go out and chop down that holly bush to show his love for me. Ha-ha. Actually, he said he would if it didn't provide privacy for the front side of the house. What I think is that he just can't be bothered. I hate brass. Jade had a boutique where almost everything was brass when I was a teenager. I just detest brass. For many years I didn't like poodles and at the time, it didn't occur to me as to why. I've overcome my problem with poodles as an animal lover. I just find it interesting that certain things that remind me of Jade also repulse me while others don't. I'm sure there's some psychology in there somewhere.

Looking back, I just can't imagine how the little things James and I did in the beginning were enough to make my dad so furious. He beat us with indignation and almost contempt. He was so big and strong yet we were so little. I remember him beating me over and over while angrily yelling that he wouldn't stop whipping me until I stopped crying. It felt impossible to stop crying. How was I supposed to stop crying when a big leather belt was whipping and welting my tender skin? The pain was insufferable but the only means to an end was to go silent. Sometimes the belt would slip and my dad accidentally hit us with the buckle. He didn't seem to notice.

The whippings became more frequent. I started wearing long sleeved shirts and pants to school because the bruises were embarrassing. I don't know if James did the same because we never talked about it. The subject was taboo. Part me hates having to share the whippings as part of this story because my dad is the sweetest, most loving man I've ever met. Unlike Jade, he really did have the capacity to love all five of us and overall, he has proven it. I know that he regrets whipping so harshly. I also know he regrets having married Jade because of what it did to Kristen, James and me. He has apologized for that repeatedly.

Once when I was 6 and James was 8, we whispered in the garage about Jade. I asked him if he thought she had magical powers. He said he had questioned whether or not she might be a wicked witch and he wondered if she could always see us no matter where we were. We concluded that we should not eat our food anymore because she was probably poisoning and trying to kill us. When my dad came home that night, she told him we were saying such bad things about her that she couldn't repeat them. She said she could only reveal one thing we said and it was that we had called her a "bitch." Curse words were unheard of in our house so this not only disappointed but also infuriated my dad. I'm pretty sure I had no idea what a "bitch" was and had more than likely never even heard the word.

I never questioned my dad's choice of punishments, I was only ashamed of myself. I often wondered if maybe he was so angry because his step children never did anything wrong. I think he was angry that his own children were apparently flawed. His step children never had to be whipped. I thought he must wonder what was wrong with us. Did he wonder if it was a genetic flaw that came through him? Maybe he was so angry because we couldn't be like Demi and Max. I know I tried with all my might to be like Demi and Jade. The difference between Demi and me was that she was comfortably floating along with the current while I was always trying to swim upstream. Jade made Demi's life as easy as possible while she tried to sabotage my every move. But unlike a salmon, I wasn't willing to die at the end of my journey and I know that I persevered over and over again.

I remember the way others received my reaction to two different movies as unusual. The first movie was "Cinderella." It seemed perfectly normal that the real daughters were dressed up for the ball while the step sister stayed home to do the chores. In the beginning, Demi, Kristen and I shared the dishwashing and other chores but eventually the chores became all my responsibility. Once Kristen moved out, Jade said that Demi no longer had to help because she had more important things to do. This was normal to me. I didn't feel sorry for Cinderella at all. Instead, I thought it was great that she had the mice to play with. I had my cats and dogs to talk to and I had a great imagination that kept me busy playing alone. I wonder if this is part of the reason I have such a love for animals; they were always there for me.

The next movie I found trivial was "Mommy Dearest" with Fay Dunaway portraying Joan Crawford. I didn't understand what was so terrible about the mother. I thought the little girl did some bad things that deserved punishment. She spoke back to her mom which I never would have done. The mom told her there were to be no wire hangers, yet the little girl used them anyway. If she didn't eat her meat, her mother would save it for the next day. I really couldn't see the problem. When I didn't eat my meat, I received whippings. I think I might have preferred having it for breakfast the next day. "Cinderella" doesn't address that the daughter is starving for a mother's love the way "Mommy Dearest" does. When I saw "Mommy Dearest" in 1981, I couldn't see how desperate the daughter was because I was just as desperate. I couldn't see how irrational the mother was because Jade was just as irrational at times and that was normal to me. Recently, I watched part of the movie again and saw it differently. There was a dramatic scene where the daughter hurtfully yet angrily scowls, "Whyyyyyy did you adopt meeeeeeeee?" I had wondered the same thing about Jade so, so, so many times. She knew my dad had three children, one of them a vulnerable teenage girl and the other two of us were so little and desperately needed a mother's love. Why didn't she give it to us? Why had she signed up for us? Did she think she would be able to love us but found that she couldn't after all? Is she mentally ill? Is there such a thing as wicked after all?

CHAPTER 8-JADE IS GREEN LIKE JEALOUSY

The jealous are troublesome to others, but a torment to themselves-*William Penn*

Jealousy would be far less torturous if we understood that love is a passion entirely unrelated to our merits-*Paul Eldridge*

In my nineties journal, I wrote, "Jade didn't like my brother James and I didn't understand why because I loved him so much. He was and would never be good enough for her."

Jade's son, Max was a huge success athletically, academically and socially. There was an eight year age difference between him and James so it didn't seem there was any reason to compare the two boys but Jade did anyway. She subtly pointed out Max's successes in the same conversations where she pointed out James' flaws. James was really too young to be compared to Max in this way and I believe it scarred him for life. He was just young and pliable enough for Jade to steer him in the direction she wanted him to go. Unfortunately, she guided him into a lifelong struggle with contempt, deception, and alcohol. In his fifties now, he is still wary of everyone and appears to think the entire world has done him a disservice.

My dad adored James, his only son by birth. It seemed Jade resented this love and her jealousy seemed to be driving her mad; so mad that she was determined to destroy James.

Jade could have won "Best Actress" for the way she waited until my dad came home and morphed into a distraught victim of James' and his terrible deeds. She took center stage and by the time she finished her monologue, my dad was so furious he whipped James until little James was red as a beet and laid whimpering on the floor. This continued for years. When my dad thought James was too old to be whipped with a belt, he began punching and slapping him.

My dad is fortunate he didn't seriously hurt James or (reluctantly but honestly I have to say) even worse. Is James as lucky? I'm guessing they would both say I'm exaggerating and I wish so much that I could believe I was. Sometimes, I wonder if because the emotional damage goes so deep, will he ever recover. Now, this is the memory that stirs my soul. I thought I had erased it for many years. Burying it didn't heal it because I can never forget that I didn't do anything about it when maybe, just maybe I could have. Now I can never know.

My dad had come home from a long day's work and Jade was waiting for him. She fabricated something terribly untrue and I could hear her wailing on and on about James doing something horrible that just never happened. I'm sure my dad just wanted her to shut up like someone with tinnitus would do anything to make the ringing in their ears go away.
I felt sympathy for James because I knew what was going to happen. I felt empathy for him because I had also experienced the impending doom and the truth I had done nothing wrong.

I heard pounding flesh and yelling through the wall. I could hear my dad smash my brother's little black and white TV and on another occasion, my dad destroyed James' stereo system. He would throw James' things on the floor and stomp on them or sometimes go out to the garage and consciously choose a mallet, walk back through the entire house to James' room and smash his belongings. He seemed to be in a thoughtless rage? Like Mr. Hide. This was NOT my dad.

This temporary stranger to me would then begin to twist James' arm backwards from his shoulder until he was in pain. Time and time again, I found myself in my bedroom pressing my hands against my ears and humming the song "You are my Sunshine" to try and drown out the noise. Finally, when I couldn't stand it anymore, I would stare at the doorknob with intentions to open it but I was always too terrified to touch it. I remember falling down with my face in the carpet crying and tasting my salty tears yet suddenly, they tasted like blood. I had bitten my lips so hard it was blood I was tasting as well. I begged God to make my dad stop hurting my brother.

I also cried because I felt like a coward. I cried because this person beating my brother was not my beautiful, sweet dad. He was a creation of a mad scientist named Jade who had temporarily transformed him. I wanted to rip open the door and scream "Stop it! You're hurting him. He's just a child!" This memory fills me with regret and saddens me more than anything else I know. Never, not once, did I ever see or hear Jade stop him and tell him he had gone too far. What was she doing in the other room while this was going on? She could have asked my dad to stop and he would have, for her. I could have asked him to stop too but I never did and I'm sorry, little James.

We all try not to live with regrets. What's the purpose? Every mistake is a lesson that makes us a better person, right? Well, not opening that door and defending my brother has never ceased to haunt me. I can't help but wonder what might have happened if I had. Friends tell me to "let it go" and that I can't go back and change it. A psychologist suggested that I might have also been beaten had I tried to intervene. I would gladly take that chance if I could go back and know that it might have changed things for James. Having done nothing trailed behind me as a ball and chain for most of my life. If I had known James would grow up to hate and distrust women, I would open the door. If I knew then that he would grow up to mistreat his girlfriends, that he would grow into a man who for many years regularly called my dad drunk late at night blaming him for making his life miserable, I would open that door, you bet I would. I would do it for my brother and I would do it for my dad because in my heart I believe that love would have broken the trance. That's exactly what it was, a trance. It was something you would have to see to understand. Jade had this power over him that temporarily transformed him. She seemed to take pleasure in our physical and emotional pain.

My aversion to physical aggression borders on hyper- sensitive. Recently, I saw a woman pushing a mentally challenged child in a wheelchair inside a grocery store. The child reached her hand out and knocked a whole row of cans off the shelf and her mother started slapping her. Stunned, I left my cart in the middle of the aisle and fled the grocery store. I sat in my car finding it hard to catch my breath.

I recently saw a man grab and twist his son's arm as they were walking through the hospital. When he was finished, I saw the boy holding his arm as if his shoulder hurt; the dad didn't even notice.

Whenever I see mothers scolding their children in public places, I bite my tongue and on occasion have said things like "what a lucky mom you are to have such a sweet child." Once I saw a man who was scolding his children for bumping his heels with the shopping cart they were pushing. When he made eye contact with me, I smiled and said, "That's why they don't get their driver's license until they're 16, they're still perfecting their motor skills." I didn't say it with sarcasm or judgment. I said it with my head tilted to one side as if admiring a cute kitten; I didn't want to offend. The man stood there stunned, staring at me as I walked away. I certainly hope I wasn't imposing and the optimistic side of me thinks I spoke to him somehow and possibly earned those sweet little children some future compassion from their father. I think of my dad and how he didn't realize the consequences of his angry actions. I didn't feel like I was being self righteous or bitchy with my little comments to random strangers. I truly tried to do it thoughtfully, in a way that might help them see but not feel judged. We sometimes forget how precious, beautiful and innocent children are. They are such a gift. Any chance I get to gently remind someone of that, I feel I owe it to little James but the opportunities are rare.

Obviously, I own some good memories of Jade. She provided me with tangible necessities and taught me useful things. This created a loyalty to her that has led me to internalize the damage she has done to Kristen, James and me and prevented me for all these years from telling this story. I wonder if my brother James has any good memories of Jade. The only nice thing I remember her doing for James was getting a speckle trout that he had caught mounted for him as a surprise. It seemed most of her kind gestures were on stage so that she could bow proudly after her performance. I'm sure there were other nice things she did for James but I can't recall one. I never saw her help him with his homework, compliment him for any job well done or hang up a piece of art he had drawn.

I never, once saw her hug him. She never hugged me either. I remember seeing mothers hug their children when they fell off their bikes or skinned their knees and finding it odd. She never once did that for me and James and I didn't miss it or long it. I found it strange. I have wracked my brain yet find a single memory of her loving James. Unfortunately I can't forget the numerous occasions where she waited with a sneer for my dad to come home. I can't erase the memories where she fabricated reasons for James to get a whipping when he hadn't done anything at all. It was terrifying and fascinating all at once.

CHAPTER 9-JAMES, DEMI, OIL AND WATER

The more whippings little James received, the worse he behaved until he was in trouble all the time. His grades were bad and he was often in trouble at school. Jade didn't want me to play with him. I wanted to but I wanted to please her just a little bit more. Because I was starving, starving for a mother's love.

James developed a terrible temper when he hit puberty. He would become angry and punch holes in the walls of his room. A couple of times he accidentally hit a beam and broke his hand. We learned how to patch up the holes so my dad wouldn't see them. If Jade or my dad found the holes, there would be hell to pay.

James never hit me, not once. He grabbed me and threw me around a little bit but probably no more than some other brothers and sisters have done. I stayed out of his way as much as I could. Although James was volatile, I wasn't terribly afraid of him in my teenage years. Sometimes on the way home from the school bus, he checked the neighbors mailboxes and stole their girly magazines.

He was a boy who did boy things. Once he caught a beautiful little fish from the canal and I asked him to please put it back gently. He laughed and raised the fish over his head and slammed it as hard as he could. It hit the water, split open and floated in pieces to the top of the water. These are the kinds of things he did often. He wasn't a rule follower and did daring things I would never think of doing. I did see him as a risk taking rebel with the potential to be dangerous. The police have shown up at our door looking for James more than once. I don't remember what he did or why they came but most things seemed to work themselves out. James probably had undiagnosed ADHD and problems with impulse control. We didn't have those diagnoses back then so he was just considered "bad." He repeated a grade somewhere along the way and ended up dropping out of school at sixteen.

At some point, James had a lovely red haired girlfriend named Valerie. For a while, Valerie brought out the best in James and it was clear that he loved her. Except for my dad, it's the only unbridled love I've ever seen him show anyone. He has always been too guarded.

James and I were only allowed to use one phone in the house and it hung from a cord in the kitchen. There was a phone in Jade and my dad's room and another in Demi's room but both of these were off limits. I had just come home from school and was cutting an orange on the kitchen counter when James suspected I was eavesdropping on an argument he was having with Valerie on the phone. He demanded I leave the room. I regretfully refused on the basis that the kitchen belonged to me too and I would leave as soon as I was finished. He slammed down the phone and barricaded me in the corner of the kitchen. His eyes were crazy and full of rage so I instinctively held my hands up as if I were surrendering to the police. I didn't even realize I had an orange slice in one hand and the knife in the other. (I never knew that our knives were exceptionally sharp because my dad was always sharpening them.) James looked at the knife and grabbed the blade. He squeezed it so quick and hard that he cut through to an artery in his hand. Blood spurted all over the kitchen and all over me. I ran as fast as I could to my room and locked the door. Several minutes later, James softly knocked on my door and calmly asked me to come out and call someone that could take him to the hospital. He told me that under no circumstances was I to tell anyone what happened. A friend of his came and took him to the ER while I sobbed and frantically cleaned up the blood. When Jade came home, I told her I didn't know where he was. Later, James came home with my dad and he was wearing a cast that was propped up in a way that would keep his hand higher than his heart. I couldn't look at him. I looked and felt so guilty. Jade strolled over to me and turned her head so that I could see her smile mirthlessly and say under her breathe "I can't believe you would do such a thing to your brother." No one spoke of it again for years except for one random comment, and I can't remember who said it; I just remember these words, "Don't mess with Kathy, she'll cut your hand off like she almost did to James!" I didn't stand up for myself then or ever. I don't know why but I sunk deeper into a state of perpetual shame.

Jade came to me once when James was 18 years old and told me he had been in a bar fight. She told me he was hiding in his closet because he was afraid that he had killed someone. She said James had left the victim for dead and was just waiting for the police to come and arrest him. I don't know how she knew this but I was terrified for James. Decades later, I question everything Jade ever said. She was a liar and she fabricated everything to her advantage. Maybe he did almost beat someone to death. I wouldn't be surprised. However, I have discovered so many fabrications and lies that I wouldn't be surprised if she completely made this story up as she did so many others. I think the truth may be somewhere in between.

James had nice friends but also had dangerous ones. In 1986, I was at my boyfriend's house watching the news. I saw James on the news testifying in court. Someone had murdered his ex-girlfriend. He was testifying about what kind of person she was. I don't remember a word he said, I just remember feeling embarrassed my brother ran with a dangerous crowd. I'd like to think I called him and asked if he was okay. I'd like to think someone was there to support him, that he had a mom he could talk to. No one ever talked about it as if it just washed right away.

Early on, I began to understand that Max and Demi were superior, James was bad and Kristen was somehow flawed. I REMEMBERED Kristen as always being slightly overweight which I wouldn't have noticed if Jade didn't constantly remind me.

Demi often called me into her room, played a record called "Chicken Fat" and made me do exercises to the music. I didn't mind and somewhat enjoyed being allowed in her room. She said if I didn't exercise, I was sure to be fat like Kristen and my birth mother. She told me I would grow big saggy breasts like Kristen as well. I know now that there was absolutely nothing wrong with Kristen or her voluptuous breasts. I recently saw a picture of her as a teenager and was shocked to see she wasn't overweight at all. She just wasn't the waif Demi was. Demi led me to believe I needed to be the skin and bones that she was and looking like her became my goal. As soon as I was allowed to wear a bra, I wore it all the time. I think I read in a Judy Bloom book that if you wear a bra to bed, your breasts wouldn't grow. I didn't want breasts because I didn't want to be like Kristen or my birth mother. I wanted to do whatever made Jade and Demi like me even though what I always settled for was unpredictable tolerance.

I always thought Kristen had a lovely face, long, silky dark blonde hair, and stunning light green eyes. However, what I found most beautiful about her was her humor. She was hysterical, so funny! I have always loved her humor. It's interesting that I remembered her as always being overweight based on Demi's impression rather than my own.

Jade taught me that Demi was a better role model for me than Kristen. She even once asked me "Do you want to be one of them or one of us?" I wish that I had understood that I didn't have to choose. I didn't understand that I was being asked to betray my sister who I had loved so much before Jade and Demi were ever part of our picture. Why did I feel so powerless? I wish that I had proudly said, "I want to be one of them!" I didn't know that I didn't have to choose in my heart. I didn't realize I had any rights at all.

A reoccurring dream I had as a child was about King Kong and Godzilla stomping through our neighborhood. They were going to stomp/crush/kill some of us but not others and it was up to me to choose who would be stomped to death. I woke up with my heart beating rapidly and feeling soon relieved it had only been a dream. I didn't relate the dream to what was happening to me psychologically, nor did I know that this choice would cost me dearly and painfully in the years to come. I wanted Jade to love me. I wanted her to love me like she did Demi. I wanted a mom more than anything in my world. Determined to win her love, I had become her little acolyte and wore blinders that obscured my peripheral view of how such subtle choices would affect my siblings.
I knew Kristen and James didn't stand a chance with Jade yet I believed there was still hope for me.

Jade cared very much about appearances and if I remember correctly, she was at one point the president of the local American Business Women's Association. The ABWA sponsored a beauty pageant in which she enrolled me when I was six years old.

She told me I was sure to win because of her clout. I innocently told the other girls in the pageant that my mom told me I was going to win. I didn't have any idea I was hurting their feelings. I wasn't Nellie Olsen from "Little House on the Prairie." I was just repeating what my new fabulous mom had told me. I didn't place. I didn't even make the top ten. After the pageant, I went backstage and hid behind a rolling hanger of dresses. I was so ashamed. The other mothers had heard that I had made the other little girls cry with my premature claim to victory. Jade came at me publicly with dramatic disdain "Why in the world would you say such a thing?!" I told her it was because she told me so. Like an Oscar winner she contorted without hesitation "I told you that no matter what, you are always a winner to me." I knew even then at six years old that she was a liar. That was not what she had told me. She told me because of her importance, I would win the pageant. These were the things I wrote letters to my dad about, letters that would be confiscated by the Jade patrol. They were enough to let her know I had seen things no one else could see and I would eventually expose her. She wouldn't let this happen.

I made good grades, I was supposedly cute enough and seemed to please Jade in the beginning.
Sometimes I would hear her refer to Kristen and James as her step children but me as her daughter. Instead of feeling sad for them, I was consumed with my need to win her approval. It was my drug and I wanted more. I tried my best to do everything just the way she wanted it. Unfortunately, around the age of eight, I really began to disappoint her. She started to call me her daughter on some days and her step daughter on days when I vitiated her perfect world.

One of my first really memorable fails was when she noticed my neck was dirty. She berated me and had me scrub it so hard that my neck turned red and my skin was raw. I still felt dirty on the inside. I felt I should have inherently known to scrub my neck. I literally thought I must have been stupid.

Max and Demi had another dad somewhere in Alabama. Demi kept a stuffed cat he had given her on her bed. It had genuine, soft, white rabbit fur, the cutest little nose and a little pink tongue hanging out of its mouth. I desperately wanted to touch it. I remember cautiously tip-toeing over to get a better look at it when she jerked it away from me and told me I would never touch her cat nor would I ever have one like it. This seemed normal because she was allowed so many privileges. I don't even remember this as if it was really eventful and mean; I just remember. Her closets and drawers were packed with new clothes and she took piano lessons. She took plane trips to see her real dad and went on ski trips with him and Max. I thought this was fascinating. Living in Florida, we had never seen snow, nor could I imagine I ever would. I never felt sorry for the rest of us, I only found her to be even more fascinating.

Early on, my family went to a pet store to get Demi a parakeet and James a hamster. When I saw the parakeets, I fell in love. My dad suggested we get two parakeets; a blue one for Demi and a yellow one for me. I was overjoyed when we brought the two parakeets home. They were each in their own little white Chinese take out box. I was allowed to hold my parakeet's box in the car and I couldn't stop peeking through the crack because he was the cutest thing I'd ever seen. I couldn't believe this tiny little life belonged to me. We set up the beautiful little domed cage that we had purchased with the birds. Demi and I were each allowed to open the cage door and gently release our parakeets to their new home.

With fascination and joy, I watched the parakeets for hours. I noticed that when I stayed very still and quiet, my parakeet seemed to blink his tiny eyes in response to me blinking mine.

Later at home, I heard my sister whining in her room and telling Jade she didn't want me to have a parakeet. Jade said in a dark voice "Don't worry, I'll take care of it." At the time, and embarrassingly for decades, it didn't phase me. The next day, I told all my friends at school about my new parakeet and ran home from the bus stop to see my bird, Sparky. He was gone! Jade told me he had fallen off his perch and broken his neck. I was temporarily devastated but recovered quickly as most children do. It wasn't until about ten years ago that a friend called me "Sparky" in jest. I told him about my bird and how he had fallen off his perch and broken his neck. My friend laughed and shook his head before replying "and you actually believed it?" That's when the memory of Jade and Demi came back to me. Did Jade kill my bird, take it back to the store or set it free? I'll never know.

Not only was I not allowed to touch Demi's vast collection of beautiful things, she refused for me to have any of her hand- me down clothes. She bagged up her clothes in garbage bags and called Goodwill to come pick them up. I literally had one pair of jeans and a few shirts. This memory is from when I was about 12 or 13 and she must have been about twenty. I mustered up the nerve to ask if I could have some of her clothes before the Goodwill truck came. She immediately snapped "No! I don't ever want to see them again, especially on you!" This was truly unforgettable.

I started babysitting every chance I could and was able to buy myself a few cute things. Jade never bought me clothes except for a few things before the school year started and for Christmas. I was always embarrassed by my wardrobe compared to the other girls at school and it never occurred to me I was deprived; I thought I was flawed and undeserving.

CHAPTER 10-WHAT IS NORMAL?

Now, here's something I wouldn't expect you to know about fish. When a flounder is first born, it's bilaterally symmetrical. It can move freely through the water like other fish. It soon begins to tilt to one side until the eye on the lower side starts to migrate to the top. That's when the flounder concedes to laying flat on one side. During this process, there are other changes to the bones, nerves, muscles and colors. It can't ever go back to being a bilaterally symmetrical fish. Those days have gone and it has transformed. Instead of swimming freely at the top of the water with the symmetrical fish, the flounder spends the rest of its life looking up. It has to shuffle around the bottom of the ocean. It also tries to blend in to the ocean floor to protect itself from harm. Does it ever remember swimming freely at the top of the water with the other fish? I'm sure it doesn't because this become its normal.

What does normal mean? According to Webster, it means "conforming to a standard; usual, typical, or expected."

My brother James liked to go gigging for flounder at night and allowed me to come along on a few occasions. We dropped the fiberglass boat off the side of the sea wall and using our trolling motor, moved quietly down the canal. He took a bright spotlight that illuminated the water and everything underneath it. It was really spectacular to see all the different kinds of sea life in this way. The flounder shuffled at the bottom camouflaging themselves in the sand. My brother would throw a spear that had a string on the end for retrieval. The flounder were everywhere. Sometimes they were so close together he would spear two at a time. If I remember correctly, he may have sold them to local restaurants because I don't remember anyone ever eating them at home. I remember my bottom and the back of my thighs would itch unbearably after going out in that boat. It wasn't until many years later that I realized it was a fiberglass boat and the tiny fiberglass particles were getting under my skin. If I had asked my dad why the boat made my skin itch, I suppose he probably would have told me and saved me a great deal of discomfort. However, we were conditioned by Jade not to bother our dad and to not ask unnecessary questions. To this day I wonder how much more I could have known and how much easier life would have been for me and my siblings if we had felt comfortable enough to ask more questions. I'm not saying we weren't ever allowed to ask questions but I know that I was often told that either my question was stupid, I talked too much, or to go look up the answer in the encyclopedia. If I asked "why" the answer was almost always a hostile "because I said so!" I spent quite some time with my face in an encyclopedia.

I heard once that if a frog is put in a comfortably warm pot of water and the heat is slowly turned up, it will just sit there and eventually boil to death because its normal changes so slowly and also because frogs are apparently not very smart. I wondered "why doesn't it just jump out?" I think the answer is because it feels normal to the frog until it becomes too late. I know people are much smarter than flounder or frogs but when something feels normal, we don't try to change it. It becomes normal for us.

Whenever I heard stories of people in abusive relationships, I wondered why they stayed. I know now that some of them stayed because they were frogs that started off in comfortable water and boiled to death before they knew it. I believe others stay because they don't realize they are being abused or think they somehow deserve it. What's normal for each of us is what's normal for each of us? My normal is what I know. Your normal is what you've experienced. His normal is the way things have always been.

I didn't consciously think about it much. James and I discussed running away on occasion but we could never devise a good plan. I continued to fantasize on my own when I was seven and eight years old. I imagined I could live on the beach between the sand dunes. I thought I could become a fisherman like "The Old Man and The Sea." I even fantasized I would befriend dolphins and swim with them holding on to their fins.

That's when my fantasies moved literally into my dreams at night. My escape was to dream about flying away and as mentioned before these were some of the most vibrant, detailed, colorful and extravagant dreams I've ever had. In 1976 when I was eight years old The Steve Miller Band released "Fly like an Eagle" which is all about flying over the sea like an eagle while solving the world's problems. I became adept at pushing back pain and waiting until bedtime when I could fly away. Sometimes if I woke up in the middle of a dream, I willed myself back to sleep so I could finish it. I stopped having these dreams in my teens and never had them again until my first son was born, in my thirties. In these dreams, my son and I could hold hands and fly together. The dreams left me again until last year when my other son was diagnosed with a critical illness. Now, I am having them again just when I need them most and in this round they are more colorful and fantastic than ever.

CHAPTER 11- JADE WEBS

At five years old, I thought Jade was perfect. She had a beautiful wardrobe, her black hair was piled high on her head like Marge Simpson's except Jade's somehow looked fashionable and beautiful. It was fashionable at that time in the early seventies. She was 5′11″ but with her hair and heels she appeared to tower over everyone else like an NBA basketball player. She carried herself well in a way that unapologetically demanded attention and she got it. She also had a way of charming my dad's friends, especially one of his closest friends, Wyatt. Wyatt was so taken by her that his wife, Janet noticed. Janet began styling her hair and trying to dress like Jade. I noticed but Wyatt never did and I felt sad for Janet because she was no contest for Jade. I started noticing this change in Janet at church and I thought no more of it than it being a compliment to Jade and a little sad for Janet.

Jade was the reason we were able to move out of our tiny house on Lindenwood and in to a nice big brick house on a canal. She came with lots of jewelry and fancy furniture. Her ex husband was an engineer for Boeing, made good investments and had some family money, I think. She must have received alimony and child support. She later justified Demi and Max having more things and being enabled to go more places because of the money that came from their other dad back in Alabama. Then, on other occasions she would publicly preach that she made a conscious effort to treat all five of us exactly the same.

I remember one Christmas she claimed to have spent the exact same amount of money on each of us. However, Kristen received an extra dollar in an envelope. Jade knew I had seen her take shopping bags full of gifts into Demi's room earlier in the day when Kristen wasn't home. This gesture with the dollar in the envelope was her "proof" to everyone that she righteously spent the exact same amount on each of us. Because she had purportedly come one dollar short for Kristen, she made a family spectacle of owing Kristen this one dollar.

This constant facade was believable to most, even to me until observations, maturity and experiences turned my eyes into a keen set of spectacles that could see things others could not.

At around the age of eight, I started writing my dad letters telling him of Jade's mistreatment and begging him to leave her. I hid my letters in the most creative places waiting for the right time and the nerve to give them to my dad. My letters always disappeared.

Once I wrote a letter to him explaining that I only had one pair of jeans and only a few shirts to wear to school. I explained that Jade never took me shopping yet she was always wearing the latest fashions and coming home with shopping bags full of things for Demi. I just asked if he could ask her to get me a few new things or let me have a few of Demi's hand me downs. I also explained much more important things in detail of which he seemed to be unaware. I told him how Jade had slapped me with fly swatters, wire hangers and small tree branches when he wasn't home. I wrote that she had accused me of awful things I didn't do so that he would whip me when he came home.

I explained I was afraid to say I didn't do these things because he would think I was a liar and whip me more. I wrote that if he had only married her so we would have a mom, then to please leave her because we were happier before Jade. I taped the letter to the bottom side of a clothes drawer in my room and went to school. Several hours later, Jade picked me up and signed me out of school. She looked sad and she sniffled pitifully in front of the school staff. She tilted her head and looked at me sadly as if she was seeking understanding. I fell for it. She took me to "the mall" which was the only shopping mall I had ever seen, therefore making it "the mall". She bought me a few pieces of clothing yet pretended this gesture was financially painful. I felt so guilty. Afterwards, she bought us lunch at a Wendy's drive-through and took me back to school. She appeared to be very sad and I felt sorry for her and I couldn't enjoy this experience at all. I came home and looked for the letter I had previously taped to the bottom of the drawer. It was gone and I wasn't the least bit surprised.

Jade always drove the latest and newest car. She had vanity plates before most people even knew what they were. Her plates were her first initial and last name. There was never a doubt that it was Jade parading her fancy new car.

Jade came to us with a little gray poodle named "Mr. French". He went almost everywhere with her. He would jump in the car and climb onto her shoulders and ride wrapped around the back of her neck. I thought this added to her elegance as it almost mimicked a fur collar. Mr. French was a part of the Jade package. He died when I was around ten years old and she laid in her bed with his dead carcass and cried for what seemed like forever. I went to the open door, the invisible boundary and I tried to comfort her. I asked her if there was anything I could do or bring to her. She just cried while her Virginia Slim cigarette burned away in the ashtray beside her. I didn't have a burning desire to run up and hug her because we had never hugged. I didn't even consciously think that laying in bed with her dead dog was weird. I just felt sad for her. The best I thought that I could do for her was to go away and let her be. That's what I did.

Jade didn't have any friends and this never seemed unusual to me until I was in my thirties. She never went to lunch or shopping with friends. No one ever came over for tea. To be exact, she had one friend in Alabama named Jewel that she would chat with on the phone for the first few years. Eventually that relationship dissolved. She seemed to be friends with her secretary at the hearing aid business that she and my dad owned. Of course her secretary was dependent on the salary that was determined by Jade and the two of them were together from 9 to 5 every day. I now wonder what their relationship really was because they only saw each other at work and there didn't seem to be any relationship once that business closed.

Jade was active in the church as far as helping with communion and cooking casseroles and compotes of banana pudding for events and new families. I believed that she was well respected and highly regarded. She did all the things the women in the church were expected to do. There were so many women she could have been friends with at church. "Why didn't she have any friends?" I often wonder.

It never occurred to me as a child that Jade might have stories about her past and childhood to share with me because it was my normal that she didn't. I never wondered about her childhood or past. It never occurred to me that she had a past at all. In my mind, it was almost as if she was a genie that had just popped out of a bottle, "Poof!" Now, I wonder why she didn't have friends, why she never told me anything about her past or her childhood; absolutely NOTHING. Why? She never read me a story from a book, she never asked me about my day, she never showed any interest in anything I loved to do. She only seemed irritated by my existence and this increased year after year. The problem was that I was addicted. I was addicted to those bones she would throw me once in a blue moon and I continued to perform for them almost desperately as a child. But when my teenage years hit, I began to become bewildered and dejected.

I began to look for love elsewhere. I thought I might find it in a romantic relationship. I thought falling in love would make everything better. I finally did fall in love at seventeen and dated the same guy until I was twenty-one. I spent most of my time at his house, with his family. This was fine with my dad and Jade as long as I showed up for church every Sunday morning, Sunday night, and Wednesday night. His father was a Methodist preacher so he and I were also required by his parents to attend his church service. We basically spent the majority of our Sundays in church. I always came home to hear from Jade that my first love was never going to heaven because he went to the wrong church. I knew in my heart this was ridiculous. So many beautiful, God fearing people were certainly not damned to hell because they didn't belong to a particular denomination and it fueled my stubborn tenacity to never conform to a religion that believed such a thing. This opinion alienated me from my dad, Jade and the church that had become my family.

Now to be fair, I FELT alienated by the church. They never stopped loving me and still love me to this day. They have been an extended family to me in a way, even though many of them have passed away or don't recognize me after all these years. I don't think they were judging me as harshly as Jade led me to believe. I don't think they thought that I was a whore if I went to the prom like she said they would; she demonized my beautiful church of loving people. I do admit that some things were questionable many years ago. I specifically remember a youth group meeting with other churches of the same denomination where we were told rock music was devil worship. They played songs backwards and claimed these were actually devil worship songs. I remember being slightly concerned but also thinking it was a little bit ludicrous. However, I trusted my church and thought that if they sent me to such an educational meeting, it must hold some truth. Only a few years later did I cognize that playing records backwards could make all kinds of sounds that could be interpreted however one might like. It also seemed that these Christian presenters magnified the parts that sounded somewhat like devil words. I have recently seen television programs that claim houses are haunted and they record sounds coming from the house. Some sort of mimic evil words, yet who knows what they are really magnifying, maybe the house is shifting or mice are chattering, yet it is manipulated to sound like demons in the house. Just like people believing Joyce Heff was 161 years old, people want to believe it. I think these church meetings were much the same. But why? What was the incentive? I never understood and I still don't yet Jade told me to listen and to listen closely. Maybe she believed it hook, line and sinker. Maybe she wasn't as brilliant and clever as I thought.

Now, wait a minute, she just was. Maybe she wasn't as refined, elegant or eloquent as I had thought, but she was definitely manipulative, clever, and brilliant in her own way. Was she a psychopath? It never, ever occurred to me that something might be wrong with her growing up. She was my normal. She was the only mom I had to emulate and she had me convinced that she was the best of everything.

Once we were all grown, Jade and my dad bought a house next to my dad's very best friend, Josh. Josh was also the preacher of our church. Our church was my parents' community and our social network. Although I never saw them together, I assumed that Jade was friends with Josh's wife Tam. I may have been wrong because that relationship ended once Jade and my dad divorced. To be fair, my parents' divorce might have been awkward for Jade and Tam as their husbands were so close. Maybe they just knew it wouldn't work out for them to remain friends or maybe they weren't really friends to begin with. I would put my money on the latter because I never once saw the two ladies together. My dad and Josh are still best friends to this day and they met forty-six years ago. I remember.

I'm not saying I think it was wrong that Jade didn't have friends. It's just hard to understand now that I have such valuable friendships myself. I can't imagine a joyful life without them. Jade and Demi were and are however, strangely close. Maybe they weren't "strangely close" to other people; maybe it was just my view. I even remember visiting as a young woman and finding it odd that Demi called Jade to tell her when she had made it home safely. She only lived a few miles away. I had never considered calling Jade to tell her when I had made it back to school when I was in college, which was a six hour drive. Maybe Demi was her best friend. Maybe she considered Demi and her little poodle as her best friends. Maybe she didn't want to make friends. Maybe she was an introvert. I wonder, "Who am I to pass judgement because she didn't have friends?" An inner voice calls back "Maybe other women could feel her spooky energy and didn't want to be near it."

Jade replaced her dead poodle with an adorable little black poodle named "Candy." Candy fell right into command. She jumped up on Jade's shoulder like a curly black sheep fur collar. Jade took her to the groomer regularly to get her nails painted and put bows in her hair. I don't remember ever once petting Candy or feeling any affection for her. I remember her crying desperately for Jade if she ever dared to go anywhere without her. I found it annoying and troublesome. I didn't know what to do about it. I guess I felt somewhat sorry for Candy yet it never occurred to me to go over and pick her up, to snuggle her, comfort her and tell her Jade would be back soon. It didn't occur to me to do these things because I wasn't allowed to touch Jade's things. Candy was Jade's thing. I've never once looked through Jade's makeup drawer, I've never worn a piece of her jewelry or borrowed even a sweater. For me, this would never be a privilege and that wasn't sad in the slightest because it was my normal.

Jade seemed to be chronically ill. I could never really see what was wrong with her. She wasn't throwing up and didn't have a fever. She just said she was sick. Coincidentally, her flare ups seemed to coincide with my dad's fishing trips. She would lay in bed and moan and cry whenever he was getting ready to go fishing. This happened quite often. Sometimes he woke me up early in the morning to tell me to keep an eye on her on his way out the door and to bring her food and drinks if she didn't come out of her room. Her episodes didn't stop him from going. He would leave before dawn and return after dusk because the fish were most hungry early in the morning and at dusk. Occasionally when his fishing buddies couldn't go, I sufficed as a last resort and he took me with him. I loved looking for gators. After dark, I could see alligator eyes all over the lake and we could hear them bellow and roar at one another. The female alligators also emitted sounds called chumpfs that sounded like cough-like purrs. My dad has the most endearing laugh and I've always loved to hear it. I learned to make the alligator sounds really, really well. He laughed as I would call to the alligators and we could see the eyes getting closer and closer to the boat. On one particular night, we watched huge eyes coming uncomfortably close to the boat. My dad's adorable laugh changed into more of a nervous giggle. A huge thump hit the bottom of our little bass boat making our boat rock so hard that water starting pouring into one side of the boat and we had to balance it out to keep it from sinking. We cranked up the motor and drove back to the landing as fast as our boat would go. My dad has forgotten this story altogether. I don't know if it's his old age or if he doesn't want to remember it because it was quite scary and he doesn't want to remember putting me in any kind of danger.

I love my dad's fishing stories. He tells the same stories sometimes because he forgets we've already heard them. Not only do my boys and I not mind hearing them but we love it. My husband and boys love to hear him laugh and he laughs all the way through his stories about owls, gators, snakes and various friends he has taken fishing over the years. He never mentions Jade being sick almost every time he went fishing. I'm sure he felt somewhat guilty but he went fishing every Saturday anyway. She always seemed to get better by the end of the day and we never missed Sunday morning church due to her Saturday illnesses.

Over the years, she told me she had one disease after another. We didn't yet have Google, so I would just listen and feel sad for her.

Once I moved out of the house, she never called me. I would have to call her every time we spoke. She would tell me about all her hardships and latest illnesses. One particular call, she told me her doctors thought she had leukemia. Apparently, they were mistaken because nothing ever came of it, thank God. I know what leukemia looks like from way too far up close and personal. Doctor's don't just suspect you have it and send you home to frighten the family. You either have it or you don't. I think she also had close calls with multiple illnesses over the years and it seemed the doctors were mistaken, time and time again. Other times she just miraculously healed from diseases and illnesses other people don't miraculously heal from.

When I was in the 9th grade, I went to a slumber party for a girl who was not in my popular group. I saw she was nervous when she gave me the invitation. When I said, "Yes," she was elated. I felt good about agreeing to go to her party and making her happy. It was one of my earliest memories of having a choice and having done the right thing. Her house was not in an upscale or even middle class neighborhood. The other girls were not from my "popular" circle but I had fun. We were running in and out of the house at dusk when I looked across the street and saw Jade sitting in her fancy Buick Riviera watching us. I pretended not to notice and shrugged it off. Later, the girls started talking about kissing and sex. They all said that they had already had sex which was shocking to me and no one I knew had even come close. When they realized I had not even come remotely close, they shoved me in a closet with my friend's little brother and told us to "do it." We fondled around in the dark with zippers and buttons and finally pretended that we were done. We were both relieved that they actually believed us and went along with the rest of the party. I didn't think it was a big deal. The next day, Jade started asking me about the party and told me that she knew what I did. This wasn't the first time I thought she was telepathic or

possibly a witch. A friend called that Saturday and Jade told her that I couldn't come to the phone. I'm not sure what else she said but she flung me a mirthless smile and sneered "your actions will have consequences." A bit later, the phone started ringing with classmates asking if I had caught herpes from having sex at the party. I was devastated and became physically ill. My stomach hurt, I developed a fever and I just wanted to sleep. I refused to go to school. I had never refused to do anything I was supposed to do before. Jade transferred me to a different school for the rest of the year and thoroughly enjoyed telling everyone see knew all about the reasons why. My life changed drastically from that day on. I felt that everywhere I went, people were looking at me like a whore with herpes. I was scared to death of going to hell for anything close to having sex. I became paranoid that if I kissed a boy or sat on a toilet seat, I might become
pregnant even though I knew better.

The next year I went to the high school where all of my old schoolmates from junior high were transitioning. I believed with all my heart that no one wanted to be friends with me. Thank God, I had met a new girl, Jordan at church over the summer. We clicked at the start and I thought we could be friends because she didn't know about my reputation. If not for her, I don't think I would have had the nerve to go back to school. I kept my head down and didn't go back to my popular crowd. I thought I was tainted. My new friend, Jordan and I didn't have the same lunch period so I just walked around the halls as if I had a purpose and was going somewhere until lunch was over. I was terrified of approaching a table and being rejected because of my "herpes." I had some friends, was invited to some parties and had some fun in high school but inside I felt like a dirty outcast. I believe that Jade is the one who started the rumor. Years later, a girl told me that she called that fateful Saturday after the slumber party and Jade said,"Kathy can't come to the phone because she has herpes." This was so long ago and I can't be sure of exactly what happened. I suppose the truth could be somewhere in the middle. I do remember how I felt and it was dreadful. Jade was always cold and distant when I needed support and nurturing. This was normal and I didn't have anything to compare it to.

Let's say she didn't start the rumor. What could she have done for me? She could have comforted me and told me to hold my head high and go back to that school. She could have called the other girl's mothers and told them to stop it. I think of all the things I would have done for my children. I have done extreme things to comfort and encourage my children. I have felt like a mother bear who could rip someone to shreds for my children.

Maybe she could have just hugged me, that would have been something too.

Sometimes when I would visit as an adult, Jade would reminisce in front of others about things I had done when I was younger. She seemed to find pleasure when she would shock me by telling other people in front of me about things that never happened. I never had the nerve to say these things didn't happen. My dad once reminded me of the time I told CPS he had hit me and they came out to our house. I never knew they came to our house and I never told them that he hit me. I didn't even know there was a CPS! Was I the one who was crazy? Did I have early onset Alzheimer's? No! I know now that Jade was gas-lighting. She told these lies in front of me. She was trying to make me think they happened. Jade fabricated awful stories about me and told them to my dad. My dad told me many, many years after the fact that I had tried to get him and Jade in trouble for tax fraud. He said that I had reported them as having claimed me on their taxes to get them in trouble. This one took me a while to figure out. I still believe, "Nothing comes from nothing" in the way that to make sourdough bread, one must at least have a "starter". Ah-hah! I remembered filling out a financial aid application for college at University of Alabama. The lady helping me asked if my parents claimed me on their taxes. I told her that

I didn't know and gave her Jade's number to call her and ask. Out of THAT came this ridiculous story my dad believed. Although he had believed I did all these terrible things and had herpes, he forgave me and loved me anyway. Yes, that's why he gets a pass where you might think I should place some blame. Sorry, I have nothing to hold against him because he loves me, he loves Kristen and he loves James. Most of all, he has never made one of us think he loves us more than the other. Even Demi and James, his love for them was there as long as they were willing to accept it.

I remember further back, my dad coming home to Jade crying. She said I had pulled all of her tomatoes off her tomato plants and lined them up in a row before they were ripe. I hadn't been anywhere near her tomato plants but my dad went into his closet for his big leather belt and beat the stress of his day right out of me.

Another time, I felt sorry for the wild little birds because our bird bath was dirty. The hose wouldn't reach the bird bath so I decided to take the top of the concrete bird bath off and carry it over to the hose. It turned out to be too heavy for me to carry, I dropped it, and it broke. Jade didn't say anything to me about it. When my dad came home, her tears started to flow and she told him I had purposely broken the bird bath just like I destroyed her tomato plants. My dad went to the closet and selected a belt that left temporary whelps on my body and permanent scars on my heart. Nope, I don't blame him. My dad believed in "spare the rod, spoil the child." Jade was his puppeteer and she exploited this belief and his Achilles heel, his temper.

CHAPTER 12- DISMISSIVE DEMI

Demi did so many nice things for me in the beginning. I think the idea of having a little sister intrigued her. She built me a doll house, but when I mentioned my barbies would never fit, she went into a rage and destroyed it.
She helped make my Halloween costumes and let me tag along with her to certain places.

I remember one St. Patrick's Day, she put tiny green footprints on the sidewalk that led to the wood pile by our fence in the backyard. That's where she left me some kind of little gift from the leprechauns. I don't remember what it was. I was still standing there delighted with my find by the woodpile when Jade pulled into the driveway in her fancy Buick. We had been told to never climb the wood pile to jump over the fence. I don't know why we were told not to do it but I never did. I was compliant and eager to please and of course, I avoided whippings. That night, when my dad came home, Jade's story was that I was climbing the woodpile and jumping over the fence when I was only following the little green footprints. I received a nasty whipping for that. A whipping for what? I know that it's hard for most people to understand why I never stood up for myself or told my side of the story. The only explanation I have is that it didn't occur to me I had the right because in my mind I didn't.

My sister (no longer my new or step sister but in my head my "sister") Demi, supposedly suffered from migraines and we were often told not to bother her. If her door was closed, we were never to knock on it. She was moody and sometimes I didn't know why she was mad at me. I also didn't understand that she was a teenager with hormones. But there were times when she scared me.

On one occasion, she became instantly mad at me and rammed her knee with all her might into my groin. Her knee went straight up between my legs and hit my tailbone. I felt a shock that resonated up my entire spine. I couldn't breathe. As I gasped for air, she looked wickedly pleased, flipped around with satisfaction and went back to her room. This was the day I became very afraid of her because somewhere in her eyes, I saw Jade.

Demi had it out for little James. She was constantly calling Jade at work to tell her what mischief and dirty deeds he had done. Demi had special food and drinks that were only for her. We were not allowed to touch them because they were for her migraines or for her urinary tract infections. James didn't care and he drank her cranberry juice right out of the bottle. She put Tabasco around the rim and in the juice so he would burn his mouth and his lips. I can't remember if I warned him or if he actually did drink the juice. I like to think I warned him because I remember feeling an urgent need to warn I absolutely feeling an urgent need to warn him but I also remember being too afraid.

Demi had a designated shelf in the bathroom. My dad boxed off the entire shelf and put a padlock on it per Jade's request. It was full of every toiletry a teenage girl could ever want. James and I shared a generic bottle of shampoo and I suppose we didn't need much more at first.

Demi didn't go away to college at first. She went to a local college and lived at home. By this time, James and I were becoming teenagers and we wanted the same kinds of things Demi had in her cabinet. We would try to squeeze our hands in between the wall and where the edges of the cabinet met to reach whatever was inside. To our surprise, our fingers were snapped with mouse traps she had strategically placed to do just that. She spent ages in that bathroom and I would occasionally get a glimpse of her toiletries and makeup lined up on the counter. She always emerged looking perfect. Eventually, my curiosity took over. I made sure that no one was home or coming home any time soon. I took off the locked latch with a Phillip's head screwdriver and opened the cabinet. I smelled the bath gels and lotions and inspected the makeup. I then carefully put everything back exactly where I found it. I was very pleased with myself now that I recall.

When I was old enough to make my own money babysitting, I started to buy my own toiletries. Never once did it seem unusual or unfair for Jade to come back from the grocery store with makeup, razors, Caress soap for Demi but never, ever for me. I was expected to buy my own. It's funny when I think back that I wouldn't dare to splurge for the pink Caress soap that Demi used. She wouldn't have wanted me to have it. She eventually tried to go away and live in a dorm at a nearby college. I don't know if she made it an entire semester or not but she soon came back home to Jade.

In high school, I tried to be resourceful and creative so that I appeared to have more clothes. A friend from church named Tabitha went to a different school and she also had a very limited wardrobe. Her father was a manager at a drug store and her mother had drowned when Tabitha was little, saving someone as a lifeguard at the beach. Her father did the best he could for her and her brother but he just didn't have the money or the time to take her shopping. Coincidentally, he looked a lot like Barney Fife from The Andy Griffith Show. When Jade spoke to him at church he practically giggled and swooned the way that Barney Fife swooned over women in the show. She loved this kind of attention. Because Tabitha and I saw each other every Sunday and Wednesday at church, we would bring the few Izod shirts we had to church in our handbags. We exchanged them twice a week so that we could expand our wardrobes. No one at school ever knew the difference because we went to different schools. Eventually, I was able to use my babysitting money to buy a beautiful little shirt. I can picture it now. It was a white button down that was designed not to be tucked in as the hem went straight across right below the belly button. It had a pretty diamond shaped design and a simple little collar. Demi noticed me wearing it and said strangely "hmmmm, that's a really cute top." I was so happy she approved and couldn't wait to wear it as soon as it came out of the wash, but I never saw my cute top again. I knew then she stole it but I didn't understand why. She couldn't wear it because I would see her. I couldn't imagine what she did with it. Maybe the top disappeared into thin air the way socks disappear in the laundry all the time. There were just so many similar events that lead me to believe it was her.

Demi was allowed to have a lock on her bedroom door. She always locked it when she left so of course I was never able to go in and look for my lost shirt. What she didn't realize is I wouldn't have gone in her room anyway out of respect and fear. Although I was afraid of Demi, I still never felt I had a problem with her and I actually believed we coexisted quite well. It's only in hindsight that I see so many things that just weren't right.

She was an introvert. She wasn't a natural beauty and certain things didn't come as easy for her as they did for me. She wasn't very popular, she wasn't a cheerleader, and boys weren't chasing after her. Jade protected her and tried to buy her happiness instead. I personally thought she was beautiful the way most little sisters admire their big sisters. She was petite, had a pretty figure and spent a lot of time on her hair and makeup. She was always tidily dressed in cute new clothes. After college she married her high school sweetheart and they are still married to this day. I think she's now a school principal and has done pretty well for herself.

As I grew older, I found Demi's life very boring and monochromatic. She went to the gym everyday and did the same routine, ate the same exact foods for breakfast and lunch, and began tanning herself dark enough that her skin became the same color as her age spots. Meanwhile I was avoiding the sun and trying to fade my pigmentation. I was trying to to express a style of my own while she was always wearing close fitting conservative clothes with tucked in shirts and always a belt. I'm not even sure I own a belt. In so many more ways, we were just different. The biggest difference was the same as Cinderella and her step sisters. Little girls need to know the step daughter doesn't always end up in glass slippers. Demi and I didn't keep in touch after she married but there were never any hard feelings between the two of us as far as I knew. It was normal for Jade to love her so much more than me. I understood that parents naturally loved their real children much more than their step children. I knew I could never adopt a child because I didn't want to love one more than the other, ever.

On one of my adult visits home, Jade started talking about how I refused her love as a child. She said she was so happy to have another little girl to love but that I never let her. She said I would freeze up or slither away from her hugs. She suggested that maybe she should have tried harder. I can't imagine this being true. Maybe "the truth is somewhere in the middle." I don't remember her ever hugging me, not once. I remember playing with the rings on her fingers during church and running my fingers along the veins bulging out of the back of her hands in the very beginning but it wasn't long before I was afraid to touch her. I wrack my brain yet can't remember her ever saying, "I love you." She did sign "Love, Mom" on cards which she only sent on formal holidays. I do know that as a young adult, I never felt comfortable when people hugged me. In fact, I hated and dreaded it. It was always awkward. I thought it was because my dad and Jade never hugged me growing up. Now I wonder if it was something more.

I hate to hear someone being referred to as "damaged goods" just because bad things have happened to them. I like to think everyone is capable of healing and happiness. However, what if there is some truth to what Jade said? Maybe I came damaged and unable to accept affection.

And maybe she's just a liar.

I've already confessed I was uncomfortable with hugs and affection as a young adult. Except with boyfriends. I absolutely loved snuggles, kisses, holding hands and all of the things that came with romantic relationships. With every boyfriend (and there were only a handful) I ran to the diving board and jumped in the deep end. Whenever I was in a relationship, I neglected girlfriends and let it consume me. I became close to my boyfriends' mothers and sisters because each time, I thought it was going to last forever. It was more than the boyfriend, it was about having a family. I wanted love and I thought finding it in a boyfriend and his family would replace what I didn't have at home. I always ended my relationships for one reason or another, especially the good ones where I was treasured and adored. Of course, I see it now. Deep down, I didn't know I was worthy.

CHAPTER 13-MAX AND DALLAS

He was around 15 when Jade and my dad married. He was the definition of tall, dark and handsome. He had super dark hair and stunning blue eyes. He played the guitar and was good at sports. He was sweet to me when I was little but we never became close because he was a teenager into teenage things. I wouldn't have expected him to care much about little girls. When we did things as a family, he was lovely and the rest of the time he was off playing football or baseball. He dated Jessica, the homecoming queen and after graduating from University of Florida, he married her.

Just like Demi, Max had lots of things: guitars, amplifier, surf boards; Jade even bought him a subscription to Playboy magazine. His college was paid for, he was in a fraternity and he had no financial worries at all. He had it all and it was Jade that made sure he did. He later landed a job as the anchorman for a local tv. Station. He turned into a local celebrity.

While the former homecoming queen was pregnant with their third child, they divorced because he confessed to having a one night stand with a stranger. He married another woman also named Jessica and they are still married to this day. I have an inkling that "she" was indeed the "one night stand."He left the broadcasting business and went into banking where he did really well.

He was living high on the hog in Dallas, Texas. I was also living in Dallas. I went to Dallas to be a flight attendant for Southwest Airlines. Jade and my dad were finally very proud of me. Back then, the interview process was grueling and less than 10% of interviewees were hired. Jade was also excited because she and my dad were going to be able to fly for free. Before training, I was going to University of South Alabama in Mobile. I had just fallen deeply in love with a gorgeous young man named Jeff.

I wasn't allowed to have my car during training so he planned to drive up my car for the flight attendant graduation and we planned to live in Dallas where I was to be stationed. He showed up right before I was scheduled to fly an eight hour shift. I knew that men were not allowed in our rooms but I interpreted this rule as meaning we couldn't have men in our rooms WITH US. I told him to wait in my room until I returned from my shift. Another student reported me and I wasn't allowed to graduate. Jade and my dad were furious. They had already driven all the way from Panama City for the ceremony. They left me there in Texas with no money whatsoever and no job.

My boyfriend's sister lived in Dallas and generously invited us to stay with her for a little while. Jeff moved back to Mobile and I was hired by Lincoln Property Company to lease apartments at "The Village." The Village was a community of over a thousand apartments divided into groups like "The Meadows" and "The Lakes." The Village was staffed with hundreds of pretty girls in their twenties. I made tons of friends and did okay because I was on commission. I was always driven by commission. I never asked my parents for money. I slept on the floor of my tiny apartment and furnished it little by little with garage sale items each time I was paid. Because I lived where I worked, I received a small discount on my rent and the company allowed me as an exception to have my rent taken out of my first check.

I went to happy hour with friends, not for the alcohol but for the free food. I went on dates just to get meals. I had some very hard times. Recently my dad told me that out of the five children, I was the only one who never borrowed money and that the rest of them never bothered to pay back their debts. He was so proud when he said this and it made the hard times worth it to hear these words.

CHAPTER 14-THE REVELATION

Once when I was really small, maybe six years old, I heard Jade and my dad arguing. I hadn't done anything wrong but the argument seemed to be about me. My dad came into my room and told me to come with him. He drove me to an ice cream shop and he looked at me very long and hard as we quietly and solemnly ate.
I had a strange feeling that he was going to send me away, to get rid of me. He drove me back home and I was relieved and shortly forgot about it.

A year or so later, Jade was angry when I asked for something. She told me that I didn't deserve to ask for anything, ever. She told me that I was a baby no one wanted and that my dad was unfortunately stuck with me. She said that no one celebrated my birth and that no one came to the hospital to see me when I was born. She said that there were no flowers, balloons or cards because my birth was a disgrace. She didn't explain why but I felt really bad and I didn't ask for much after that. A six year old doesn't ask "what was disgraceful about me?"

Another day she was complaining about having to buy my cheerleading uniform. She told me that I only wanted to be a cheerleader to bend over and shake my ass for the boys. I loved cheerleading so much that I would practice hours on end using the reflective glass of our sliding glass door as my mirror. I wasn't allowed to take gymnastics but self taught myself front walkovers, back walkovers and handsprings. As a matter of fact, my dear friend Ari who lived across the street took gymnastics, ballet and tap. She would come home from class and we would dress up in her pink leotards and she would teach me what she learned in class.

Demi had been worthy of ballet, tap and piano lessons but I never questioned why I was not.

I wanted to be a Girl Scout Brownie. I would tag along to Belk Hudson's department store with Jade to pick up her designer clothes and makeup. I was drawn like a magnet to the Girl Scout counter where all of the badges were on display. The Girl Scout uniforms and Brownie uniforms could be purchased there. I finally found the nerve to ask if I could please be a Brownie. Jade retorted, "There's a reason why they're called Brownies. Only lower class white girls and black girls are in the Brownies or Girl Scouts!"

Jade surprisingly continued to let me cheer, came to the games and seemed to support me and even on occasion seemed somewhat proud of me. When we were alone, she would talk about cheerleading as something dirty and wrong. I continued to cheer for many years. I remember cheerleading as one of my refuge away from my increasingly unhappy home. Other times, she told me my destiny was to grow up to be a whore like my birth mother. She told me that I would grow up to be fat.

Once she told me if she and my dad hadn't been stuck with me then they could do more for their "real children." I was puzzled but didn't ruminate on it. Other days she would tell me I didn't belong. She asked me, "Don't you ever wonder why you're not like anybody else in this family; you don't even look anything like Kristen or James?" She reminded me "They have blue and green eyes while yours are a strange yellow." It still wasn't until she said, "You're just like Edgar Abernathy that I really started to piece all of these statements together. Edgar was my uncle, married to my dad's beloved sister, Trina.

We went to visit them about once a year growing up. They lived on a big piece of property where my dad's mother had a pale yellow trailer strategically placed in between my dad's two sisters' houses. I was 17ish when I finally pieced together that I must have been an illegitimate baby. My birth mother had an affair and became pregnant with me. Who did she have an affair with, Edgar? Was this why no one wanted to see me at the hospital? It all made sense. My birth mother had an affair with my dad's brother in law. Why did Edgar and my dad's sister stay married for the rest of their lives yet my birth mother was cast away as a cheating whore? Why didn't anyone tell me? Why did they let me visit my uncle Edgar, sit on his lap, play on his CB radio all the while not knowing he was my birth father?

Who knew? Did the aunts and uncles know, did my older brother and sisters know all along? The answer is "yes" everyone knew except for me. The revelation was not long before the day I went to the salon where Kristen worked and when Kristen told me about my birth mother.

Jade and my dad had been yelling at me about something the day before. I blurted out, "What do you care, You're not my real dad anyway!" My dad looked shocked and asked who told me. I nodded my head toward Jade and said, "She did." She came at me, grabbed me by the hair ripping the hair from head and screaming "you little liar!! How dare you? I would never!" I don't remember what happened after that but he believed her. He always believed her. I do remember this, though. Jade never lost her temper and everything she did was cold and deliberate. She had to perform this shocking rage and to me, she was as transparent as freshly cleaned glass.

Kristen believes she raised me on her own until my dad married Jade. I'm sure she did help take care of me but yet we had a full time nanny, Betty who I clearly remember taking care of us while my dad was at work. I loved Betty more than all the world. She came as a significant part of our package when my dad married Jade but it wasn't long before Jade disposed of her. Betty was valued as a beloved grandmother by Kristen, James and me. Jade discarded her like garbage. I wish Jade had never seen how much we loved Betty and how much she loved us. I believe Jade was afraid Betty would love us more than she would care about Demi and Max and that was something she couldn't allow. I don't necessarily blame Jade for that. However it was a painful loss and I worried about what happened to Betty and I missed her for years to come. I know she is dead and gone now and I never told her she was so important to me or how much I loved her. My dad took me to visit her in my early teens and I felt overwhelmed. I didn't know how to tell her how much she had meant to me and I wanted to cry. I pushed my feelings back and moved on.

Kristen was about 9 years older than me. She was a teenager by the time our dad married Jade. She remembered clearly our happy life before Jade and she also remembered our birth mother. She was forced into a new family with a new step sister with whom she was to share a room. Jade enjoyed introducing and providing Kristen with the teenage luxuries she had never had in the beginning. However, once the novelty wore off, Kristen acquired part time jobs and was expected to buy her own things. Demi also had part time jobs for a while yet it seemed she had more of everything; not just material things, privileges, affection, praise and even my dad. My dad won Jade's affection with his attentiveness to Demi while Kristen, James and I could no longer break through the invisible barrier between us.

Kristen didn't go to college. She went to cosmetology school instead. She always seemed fragile...damaged. She was a teenager when I was a little girl and began to take little interest in me and this I believe was typical of most siblings with vast age differences. I don't know what her relationship was with Jade. I found out later that it was also abusive much like mine except for the occasional physical abuse she saved just for me. We were conditioned not to talk to each other. It wasn't until I was eighteen years old that I went to see Kristen at the hair salon where she worked. I was discouraged from talking to her at all except when it came time for a free haircut. During the haircut, I began telling her about some of the mental abuse and the hateful things Jade would say to me when no one was around. Kristen became very angry. She told me that she had been in touch with our birth mother, Annie all along and that the poor woman couldn't sleep at night over having lost me. She said my birth mother would come and see me in a heartbeat if only I would say the word. I felt so guilty and so sorry for our birth mother. I felt as if I had broken this poor woman's heart. I had to make it better and I agreed to see my birth mother. I was nervous, guilty and I felt like Peter betraying Jesus all over again.

Annie came to see me and brought three girls who were apparently my half sisters. The first was named Paulina after the rooster, Paul who I remembered her dating and cock-a- doodling when I was 4 or 5 years old. Paulina reminded me of Kristen, my oldest sister. The second daughter was named Geneva whom Annie had conceived with some other man. Geneva was some female version of that man's name. Geneva reminded me so much of my older brother James in ways and appearance. The youngest of the three was a pretty little girl named Brandy. Brandy seemed the most like me. I couldn't help but think, "You literally replaced us all and in order!" Paulina was a duplicate of Kristen, Geneva was like James and Brandy was much like me.

I asked why she named her youngest child "Brandy." She said it was from a 70's song by Looking Glass about a beautiful bartender. I couldn't believe that while I had been sitting in the back seat of Jade's car listening to that song and visualizing a beautiful Brandy, she was replacing me with one.

She confirmed that Paulina was named after Paul. She explained the meaning of Geneva's name which I don't remember. That's when she asked if I wanted to know about my name. She told me Kathryn came from her name and that my middle name was (I will never reveal what it was.) She explained I was her love child from an affair she had with my dad's brother in law, Edgar and she came up with my middle name after him.

Over the years, she had changed her name from Annie to Kathy. To hear people call her "Kathy" made me feel so strange. I had always been told her name was Annie; my name was Kathy. I felt strangely violated by her changing her name to Kathy and by naming me after someone I didn't even know was my biological father. Why did she name me after someone she had an affair with? I was so confused yet I stayed with her for several weeks trying to get to know her and forge a relationship.I wonder how many times Annie was married. She had 6 different children with 5 different men. I just absolutely couldn't relate to her at all.

Why was she suddenly going by Kathy? It didn't make sense to me and I started to hate the sound of it. I still do. I cringe when anyone calls me "Kathy," except for some family members and childhood friends who are tenured to get a pass. The day I met Annie with her girls, they ran up to me and hugged me and said they had waited their entire lives to meet me. Annie had school pictures of me in her house. I felt betrayed by Kristen for allowing this strange woman access to my life without my knowledge. I imagined her sneaking pictures each year and sending them in the mail to her. It was all incredibly strange. My birth mother hugged me and said she loved me. I didn't love her. I didn't even know her. I didn't like the way she looked, talked or presented herself. I remember she was carrying a silver purse and it was so ugly. Why did I care about her silver purse? Why didn't I like the way she looked or carried herself? There was nothing wrong with her. She just wasn't Jade. I was disappointed and I felt guilty and weird that she wanted an instant relationship. I didn't. I thought about the talk shows I had seen where people were reunited with their long lost parents or children.

I remember seeing how miraculous it was for them on TV. They were overjoyed and cried happily. Why didn't I feel this way? I felt as if I was betraying Jade and my dad. I felt awful.

CONFRONTING EDGAR-CHAPTER-15

Edgar was married to my aunt Trina, my dad's sister. They had two daughters and a son. My birth mother said that I was her and Edgar's love child and that they had both agreed to take me as soon as I was born and escape together. Unfortunately for Annie, Edgar changed his mind. Trina wanted to forgive her husband and stay married and my dad wanted his sister to be happy. It was easier for everyone to concede that my birth mother had lured and seduced Edgar. A book called "Wicked Siren" by Eliza Lloy came out in 2015 about a diva named Viviana Love who did what she had to do to get by. She had an inconvenient marriage and seduced other men. She gave up a child and hid her past so that she could have a better life. Is this what had happened?

During my short lived and attempted reconciliation with my birth mother, she told me some of these things. She also said she didn't give us up, that my dad had taken us from her at gunpoint. This still doesn't explain why he gained custody of us.

I could see that my birth mother's heart had never completely healed from her affair with Edgar. She said he owed me the truth and should probably give me some money. She used this as an excuse to contact him and drove me to his house to confront him. The drive to his house and the drive home are a blur and I don't remember feeling anything.
I remember the details of being there as if they are carved in my brain. I walked alone up to the kitchen door inside the garage where we always entered and exited on our summer visits. I knocked on the door. He opened the door and stared at me in surprise. I just stood there. He said, "Kathy? What are you doing here?" I asked him, "I want to know if you are my father?" He looked very uncomfortable and said he couldn't have this conversation at the moment. He said, "For heaven's sake my grandchildren are here!" He could see I wasn't going to leave. Then he hesitated and told me to meet him down the road.

My birth mother drove me down a dirt road lined with pink blossoming Crape Myrtles. This is the same road where I had always gasped with glee when I saw the Crape Myrtle trees because I knew we had finally arrived to Grandma's house and we didn't have pink trees in Florida.. Edgar's truck came barreling down the road throwing up dry red clay and gravel as he slammed it into park. I climbed up into his passenger seat. He looked annoyed. He shook his head and said, "You're the prettiest girl I've ever seen in my life." He hung his head down low and began shaking it side to side. He then looked up at me with his chin still low and said, "But I ain't your daddy. You see, your momma was a whore. Hell! Your daddy could have been any truck driver passing through town for all we know. I ain't your daddy." I morphed into a bull with steam coming out of my nostrils, I retorted, "You're right! You're NOT my daddy! My dad's name is James and he's in Panama City. Nothing will ever change that." I jumped down out of his truck and slammed the door. Before I knew it, Edgar had called my dad and told him I came to him looking for money. My dad was furious with me and it seems we didn't speak for a while. If I had it to do over, I probably wouldn't have gone yet if he had nothing to hide, he would have invited me for tea and told the family about my silly notion. Whether what Jade told me and Annie confirmed is true or not, he clearly had the affair and that's why I didn't get any tea.

After that I tried to have a relationship with my birth mother, I even tried to stay and live with her after that falling out with Jade and my dad; I felt I didn't have anywhere else to go. One day while visiting Annie in Alabama, my sister Kristen came to me and said, "We know this is uncomfortable for you and 'Mother' doesn't want you to feel you have to be in this relationship with her." I said, "Thank you," I picked up my things and left.

I never saw my birth mother again and I can't recall what she looked like. I went to college and changed my name from Kathy to Kathryn because I felt Kathy had been taken away from me. I never, ever told anyone my middle name ever again and when I married, I replaced it with my maiden name.

My dad and I have always had a way of avoiding unpleasant conversations. I found out recently that if my dad ever received a letter he was afraid might say something unpleasant, he just didn't read it. I laughed when I heard this because I tend to do the same thing. It seldom happens but if I'm afraid someone is going to say something hurtful, I avoid it at all costs. My dad and I have never discussed the whipping and we have never discussed Edgar.

A psychologist once asked me, "Why don't you ever blame your dad? He went to the closet, chose a belt and took out his anger on you. He chose to turn a blind eye to the neglect, mind games and torture you stepmom was inflicting on you? Couldn't he see you had no clothes, couldn't he see the difference in the way Jade treated you and the way she treated Demi?" She told me I needed to hold him responsible. That was twenty years ago and I have given it a great deal of thought since then. I've chosen not to hold him accountable despite this advice.

For one reason, I think of the song by Michael Bolton called "When a Man Loves A Woman." He explains it so very well. He sings that a man can't see that his woman is bad and he would turn his back on his best friend for her. He sings that she can do nothing wrong in his eyes. He goes on to sing about her playing him for a fool and bringing him misery but yet he never even realizes it as long as he has her. For many years I've heard this song and each time, I thought of my dad. I've forgiven him over and over again because of the words to this song. How can I blame him for truly loving a woman and for wanting us to have a mother? He was never cruel to me in his words or actions other than brutal whippings provoked by Jade. He believed with all his heart he was doing the right thing. I know this to be true and I also know he regrets it.

When visiting him many years later as an adult, my oldest son was just a toddler and acting up at his house. My dad threatened to go get his belt. With daggers shooting from my eyes I declared, "You will NEVER lay a hand on my children!" He froze and I could see that he remembered and he knew what he had done to me and how it had hurt me so deeply. Since he divorced Jade and learned of the things she had done and said to us, his ocean blue eyes filled with tears as he apologized for not seeing it. I don't want to talk to him about the whippings.

The Jade-less man I know now is the same dad who loved us so dearly and raised us by himself when we were little. He's actually a better man now. He's suffered, not only himself but he still suffers from seeing the damage Jade has done to his three children's' lives. He will never hit me again, he will never hit my children.

He's eighty years old and loved by so many people. It may have taken him sixty years, but he finally married a wonderful woman and embraced her children with as much love as he tried to give Demi and Max. He has enough room in his heart to love all of us whether we are blood or not. He laughs hard and often. He has earned the respect of intelligent people even though he never went to college because he exudes a different kind of intelligence; one that comes from hard work and life experiences. Children love him and he sincerely cares about others.

When I think of him, I don't think about the Jade era neglect or whippings. I think of the times beggars would stand outside our church and he talked to them and then we walked across the street to Kentucky Fried Chicken and bought them a meal. They were usually men and my dad would treat each one with dignity.

I think of him never denying me a stray cat that I had found and wanted to keep, letting us have candy any time we went to the store, or the way my children adore him. I think of the times he took me fishing and put up with my girlish ways. He would laugh when I couldn't bear to hook worms or minnows. I think of the time he built me a booth for my puppet shows and didn't get mad when I had my first fender bender. I think of the look in his beautiful blue eyes each time we say goodbye. He looks into my soul and with those eyes he says, "I really love you. I'm sorry. I'm proud of you and I know this could be the last time I ever see you." I believe he knows that my eyes are saying the exact same thing back to him.

In a speculative conversation with a psychologist friend of mine, she mentioned a term called Alexithymia. It involves a lack of feelings and inability to express them. Maybe, like Autism, it has a spectrum. Maybe Jade is on it and just maybe so am I. I began telling this story about a perceived monster; a mean, evil woman who abused my siblings and me and someone who affected the outcome of our lives by leaving us to be nothing more than "damaged goods." The beautiful, fascinating outcome is that I don't see her that way any more. Maybe she couldn't relate to certain emotions because she has never experienced them. Is that her fault? I have concluded through deep reflection, seeking understanding and consulting with professionals that many of her behaviors and actions were based on jealousy. It took me so long, decades to come to this conclusion. I believe it's because I don't understand what jealousy feels like. I thought I did once. I thought I was actually insanely jealous of my first boyfriend's exes. I understand that now as fear. I had very idealistic views on intimacy and apparently he had not. I was just afraid they shared something with him that I had not. Jealousy is different and I just don't get it. Does that mean I have some form of Alexithymia? Or is it a blessing?

Somehow, I feel grateful I don't suffer from jealousy but then again, it makes it hard to understand why other people do hurtful things to each other because of it. Maybe Jade has some other kind of mental condition I don't understand like bipolar or maybe she is a psychopath. I don't wish for her to be any of these things or anything less than happy. I just tried to solve this mystery because I suppose I thought it would help me gain a healing, understanding. Instead, I believe it's accepting the unexplained for what it was and find the blessing in it is what holds the cure. It's been almost thirteen years since I have seen her. The last time I visited her, I asked if she had a good relationship with her mother or if something bad had happened to her. She looked at me as if I had just sprouted a tail. She said ,"No, I had a great relationship with my mother." I thought it was clear I was really asking, "What made you this way?" but she really didn't seem to understand what I meant. In hindsight, I wasn't presenting her with a riddle as she had done to me my entire life. I was truly, honestly JUST seeking understanding.

I spent my teenage years and young adult life floundering around literally just trying to get by and periodically I would revert to that stray dog begging Jade for a bone yet knowing I might get kicked away. Not only was she verbally and emotionally abusive when I was a child, she continued to abuse me as an adult and I refused to acknowledge it. She lied about me constantly and consistently. In my twenties, I remember standing outside the church when I was visiting Panama City. Another young woman I didn't know came rushing up to me. She said, "Oh you're Kathy! I've heard so much about you. I was so impressed to hear that you were a flight attendant but I just can't believe you got yourself fired for having sex with boys in your room. Silly!" I walked away in disgrace and disbelief.

Several years earlier, I was going to school at the University of South Alabama in Mobile. I had an abnormal pap smear and was scheduled to have a few pre cancerous cells removed. Surprisingly, Jade came to Mobile for the procedure and was very dramatic about the whole thing. This is one of the only times I ever remember her visiting me. But now, of course! I see it was an opportunity for her to play a heroin and make me look bad at the same time. Bonus points! Afterwards, she went back to Panama City and told everyone I had precancerous cells and that they were caused by having too many sexual partners.

My dad slowly and steadily became more and more distant over the years until we were hardly talking at all. By the time I was in college we only spoke through Jade and when we did, he seemed to hold contempt for me. Jade paid for my first year of junior college and I lived at home. I also had a full time job at a department store in the mall as I was saving to go to University of Alabama the following year with my boyfriend. My grades were sub par at my junior college and Jade said she and my dad would no longer help me with college tuition, housing or even car insurance. She knew without question I wouldn't say anything to my dad. I never, ever had before. I assumed the mandate had come from my dad and didn't question it. I had terrible organizational and study skills and zero direction or support from my parents. They were consistently inattentive to my education but tyrants about my grades. Jade had taken me for a psychological evaluation when I was in elementary school because she noticed I wrote and drew many things upside down and/or backwards. She was told I was indeed dyslexic but also gifted and I would grow out of the dyslexia. She often told me that it was time I grew out of it but I couldn't. Sometimes when reading a book, I couldn't remember what I had read because I transposed entire syllables. When doing a long division problem, I would often switch to multiplication or subtraction. When riding my bike in our very familiar neighborhood, I would suddenly become lost and not remember which direction I was coming from. It wasn't until I was an adult that I was reevaluated and told I never had dyslexia to begin with. Instead I supposedly have something called Cross Dominance which has more to do with using one hand for certain tasks and the other hand for others; this can confuse the brain. I don't blame Jade for believing it was just dyslexia and that I would grow out of it. Apparently many children do. However, if she were actually attentive to my education rather than my grades, she could have helped me or checked my homework. She could have looked into why my grades started to deteriorate as I grew older. Instead of putting me on restriction for an entire grade period for bad grades, she maybe could have asked why I was suffering at school. I truly tried my best but somewhere along the line gave up. I went to college anyway and I took out loans to go to school in Tuscaloosa so I could be with my boyfriend. I wanted to cheer and go to The University of Alabama. Let's just say that didn't work out. I went to a junior college near the University where my boyfriend attended. I had jobs waiting tables and teaching aerobics. I went to all the football games and fraternity parties with my boyfriend but my grades suffered miserably. I was lost, I was floundering. When I came home to visit, I felt my dad and even sometimes Jade seemed happy to see me but they were always somewhat disappointed and it showed. It wasn't until Jade was gone and I was a grown woman that I learned from my dad that all those years I struggled through college, Jade was telling him they were paying my tuition. He never understood why I was doing so poorly and he was angry with me. He just didn't know what to say or do. He never went to college and barely graduated from high school. Although he was offered a potential football scholarship at Southern Mississippi, his father died and he chose to work and support his family instead. How was he supposed to understand or help me through understanding college? He just knew that Max and Demi didn't have any problems graduating from college so he wondered what was wrong with the other three of us.

CHAPTER 16-PREDICTIONS

When I was in my late twenties, my dad called me to tell me that he and Jade has separated. He sounded so sad and heart broken. We started having long, lingering conversations on the phone almost every night. Mostly I would listen. Although I was heartbroken for him, it was bittersweet for me. I was slowly getting my dad back, even if it was only going to be for a short time until they reconciled. I treasured these talks. He had spent more than 25 years with Jade and thought they would grow old together. I felt so incredibly sad for my dad. I didn't think about all the pain she had caused Kristen, James and me. I didn't want them to divorce. I just wanted my dad to be happy.

I decided that when I came home for the holidays, I would stay with Jade and talk some sense into her. I came home to a different Jade. She wasn't her usual calm, cold self. She had lost a great deal of weight. I thought she looked good except she was jittery and aloof. She kept leaving the room and whispering on the phone for long periods of time. I just assumed she was whispering about me to Demi as she often did. She cooked her usual Thanksgiving meal and left it for me to serve because she didn't want to be there when my dad arrived. Demi didn't come for the first time. I don't remember if Max and Jessica #2 were there. I just remember trying to carve the turkey and get everything on the table before it was cold. I don't know if it was the task at hand, the strange energy or the weight of my dad's broken heart but I could barely handle it. I felt dizzy, nauseous and overwhelmed. It was an awful feeling.

I came back for Christmas and Jade was even thinner and even more elusive. I told her my dad loved her so much and pleaded with her to take him back. She wouldn't listen. One night during this visit, I had to take her to the ER to get an IV because she was so dehydrated she could hardly walk. I felt awful for her and I don't know exactly why Demi wasn't there for her except I suspect that this was a performance. I sat there with her for hours and I wanted to help her. I didn't ask her any more questions about the separation. We were the only two people staying in the house that Christmas. James and Kristen refused to have anything to do with her and their resentment toward me was growing like a weed.

As I was leaving to go back to Texas, my dad told me Jade had been having an affair with one of his business partners and a long time friend from church. That person was Wyatt, the very man from church who had always been enamored by Jade. Ah-hah, I knew it! I had seen it many years before when his wife tried so hard to look like her. My dad was grief stricken. Shortly thereafter, Jade gave most of her furniture and some of her jewelry to Demi. She moved into an apartment and bought all new furniture on her and my dad's joint credit cards. She took out a second mortgage on their home somehow and stashed money away where my dad couldn't find it or prove it. She was always very clever. They divorced and my dad was left deeply in debt. To be fair, she has her side of the story too but I SAW my dad deeply in debt. I saw my dad have to move to another town to open up another hearing aid business all by himself. He had to move away from his town, his church, his friends and his community. He had signed a non-compete when they retired and sold their business together. He had to struggle because of the divorce. The divorce that was not his choice.

CHAPTER 17-WYATT

Wyatt had eventually done well for himself in construction and Jade married him not too long after she divorced my dad. I thought back to a time when I was six years old and Wyatt came to my dad for a job. He was new at our church and in a very bad place financially. My dad taught him how to sell hearing aids. Wyatt did well, worked hard and saved up enough money to open his own construction company.

They remained good friends for twenty years. I was always proud of my dad for giving Wyatt his start. That was until Wyatt stole his wife and the only mom I had worked so hard to win. When Kristen and James found out about Jade's betrayal, they quickly and easily disowned her. I could not. I continued to visit her when I came to town and I tried to split my time between my dad and Jade. Sometimes I was afraid to tell my dad I was going to see her so I did it secretly. He usually found out and felt betrayed by me. Kristen and James began to hate me. I tried to explain "they divorced each other, not me. God says to forgive, my heart says to forgive and not to judge." They couldn't understand how I could forgive her and how I could stand to see her.

Whenever I came to visit, Wyatt was always conveniently out of town which I appreciated. I didn't want to see him but I didn't hate him. I didn't understand him but I felt indifferent to him and I still wanted Jade to be happy.

I don't know at what point I started to realize I was like a stray dog that kept coming to Jade hungry for food. Half the time, I would get kicked away but the other fifty percent I knew I just might get thrown a bone. I was so desperate for that bone that I endured the proverbial kicks. They hurt so bad but I was still starving for those tasty bones tasted so and I knew if I begged just right, there was always a chance I might get another bone.

CHAPTER 18-GIFTS FROM JAMES

My brother James has given me three tangible gifts in my life time. One, was when I was seven, we drew names for a Christmas Eve exchange and James received my name. He gave me some puffy white crocheted mittens and I hated them. The gift exchange was on Christmas Eve and was the one and only gift we were allowed to open. Wanting immediate gratification, of course I had hoped for a fun toy, not mittens in Florida. Looking back, I feel bad that I didn't like the mittens and that I showed it. I want to go back and tell that little boy that I loved the mittens he had chosen for me because HE gave them to me.

I want to tell him this as the truth. I wish I had the emotional maturity to love the mittens because he gave them to me. He of all people needed to feel that he was enough. Instead I knew Jade would tell me to wear the mittens that night when we went Christmas caroling so I hid them. Everyone was hustling to get out the door and I knew I had to be quick. I was sitting next to a lamp so I put the mittens on top of the light bulb inside the lamp and said I couldn't find them. An hour later, the lamp caught on fire and the mittens were found. I'm sure James's feelings were hurt.

The second gift he gave me, I was in my twenties. Jade and my dad were still together and we all came home for Christmas. James was temporarily doing quite well for himself in one of his numerous business ventures. I think he wanted us to be proud of him and for the first time as adults, he gave all us nice gifts. Mine was a George Foreman grill. I wish I had told him that I proud of him. I didn't and the reason why was because I didn't want Jade to see me speaking to James at all. By this time, she had grown to despise him.

He and Kristen were standing outside smoking when I walked by. He contemptuously questioned "What's wrong, Kathy? Are you too good to hang out with us?" I nervously replied that I had something to do inside. Why didn't I stop and chat with my brother and sister? Instead I went back inside and kissed Jade's ass as usual. I knew there was growing dissonance between James and me and I didn't know how to stop it.

The third/last gift James gave me was a book that he Fed Exed me the first Christmas after my parents divorced. It was called "Don't Be Manipulated." I was confused and gave it away. I was convinced I was doing the right thing. James could see I was still being manipulated and he was trying to tell me to stop.

Before the divorce, James would bring girlfriends home while conspiratorial whispering could be heard coming from Demi and Jade in the kitchen. We never made them feel welcomed. I made minimal small talk with them but I'm sure I seemed somewhat smug. James' relationships with women never worked out. I think it's because deep down he hates women. The same psychologist that told me about Kristen being hurt by our birth mother's abandonment also asked me to consider what James went through as a child. You might be thinking, "But she didn't abandon you, you were taken from her..." In our hearts she abandoned us. I always wondered why she never tried to get us back. Not only does James feel abandoned by his birth mother, he was raised by a woman who hated him. Jade hated him because she was jealous of him. He didn't know that. He just knew that she was evil and that she hated him. Why wouldn't he grow up to hate women? And me? I didn't help much. I always chose Jade over James and Kristen. I always chose to be in the kitchen with Demi and Jade as they gossiped about my brother in the next room.

James had various jobs where he would thrive for a while and then hit rock bottom. He at least, would get up and find some kind of manual labor like construction or truck driving. He would very often show up on Thanksgiving or Christmas Eve with some poor soul from one of his jobs that had nowhere else to go. He knew there would be a good meal and if it was Christmas, Jade would send me out to buy a quick gift for his friend. Though we went through the motions, her heart wasn't in it and she complained behind his back about the burden he put on her when he did these things. She spoke of it as if he was selfish and inconsiderate. Instead, I really do think that he was being kind and I wish I had done more to make his many guests feel more comfortable. He finally brought home a girlfriend who was pregnant and they were to get married. She was extraordinarily quiet and seemed simple and incapable of and disinterested in substantial conversation. I left the gossip in the kitchen to sit with her on the couch because whether we liked it or not, she was going to be in the family. I asked if she had a name for the baby. She said she was going to be named Nala from the movie "The Lion King." Jade and Demi later snickered at what a stupid name they thought it was; I played my designated role and agreed.

James took Nala from her mother when she was a toddler and raised her by himself just like my dad did with us. He said the mother was unfit and he had to do this in Nala's best interest. I presume she wasn't an ideal mother based on facts that are irrelevant here but I also think that he thought this would make our dad proud. He could follow in his footsteps in this way. There were many things I saw my brother do while raising Nala that worried me. He made her ride in the car when he was drunk. He left her at home alone with no food for days at a time. I don't care to dig up all the reasons, but I was concerned for her. I wanted her to come and live with me and I wanted to take care of her. I wanted to help my brother but was too afraid to ask because I knew he had grown to hate me.

I don't know how old Nala was when her mother died. She hadn't known her but James took her to the funeral for closure. I admired him for that. We found out later that she had been murdered and that it was drug related. It broke my heart for Nala to have to remember her mother in this way.

CHAPTER 19-LOSING KRISTEN

Kristen's first husband turned out to be gay and they divorced. She put on a great deal of weight in her twenties and has spent thirty years losing it and gaining it back again. Throughout the years, I never knew what I would come home to. One year she would be involved in some religious cult and the next year she would be drunk my entire visit. The only consistency was that she never had any money. She eventually married and divorced seven times; yes seven. I kept hoping she would realize that maybe marriage just wasn't her thing.

A psychologist told me that the age at which a child is abandoned is very critical. She told me that Kristen remembered her birth mother and had a relationship with her which could have been more devastating and insurmountable for her. Kristen and I stayed in touch over the years until twelve years ago when I learned how she really felt about me.

I had always wanted my big sister to be proud of me. I was fortunate/lucky/blessed to have a good job while she lived paycheck to paycheck as a single mother to Chelsea and Lily in between her seven marriages.

When I went to visit, I paid for things, bought clothes for Chelsea and eventually started sending her my clothes that I didn't wear anymore. I made really good money but had worked hard for it. In Kristen's mind, I threw it around and made her feel bad. My intention was to make her proud of me. She never asked to borrow money but I wish that I had given her however much she needed. Before I married, I came to visit her in Tallahassee. She picked me up from the airport and said that there was no food in the house. If we wanted dinner, we would have to stop at the store. Of course, I paid for the groceries and she said she wanted a bottle of wine. I picked up a standard size bottle of wine. She said, "Oh, that won't be nearly enough!" She grabbed another oversized bottle. At the time, I thought it was funny. I was happy to be with my sister and happily bought the extra bottle of wine.

I couldn't find any flatware or plates in her tiny, one bedroom apartment where she and her two daughters lived. She pulled out a handmade ceramic platter I have given her many years before that had a quote about sisters painted on it. It had the tiny little holes in the top as it was intended to be hung on a wall. She proudly told me that she ate her dinner on it every night and didn't really have any other plates. I don't know if she could see the disappointment on my face when I saw her eating off what I had purchased as a piece of art. I guess I wanted what I thought was "more" for her and I really don't know if she saw the disappointment in my face. I wasn't disappointed in her. I was disappointed in the reality versus the intentions I had set. I had expected to see it hanging on the wall. Although I would go back and handle the situation much more gracefully if I could, I'm approaching a place of indifference after all these years of repeated rejection. I don't remember why we found ourselves in an argument later that night but somewhere she said, "Why do you even come home?" Regretfully, I held up my hands as if to say, "Look around you" and I said, "Well look what I have to come home to!" Chelsea started to cry and pleaded with me not to leave. We calmed down, apologized and I stayed. The next time I came to visit was to see Kristen's new baby, Lily. She had married again in her 40's because she was having a baby. I was happy for her and we had a great visit. I made a special trip to be with her when she had the baby and I thought this particular trip went very well. A few years later, we met in Panama City. I was married but had quit my job to travel abroad with my new husband. Kristen yelled at her children and revealed an explosive temper. I never saw her hit them but her voice was deep and guttural when she was mad and it made me uncomfortable. I thought the things that yelled at them for were not so bad. I mistakenly asked her to please not yell at them so much. This infuriated her and she told me I could place judgement once I had children of my own. She was probably right about that and I am super sensitive when children are yelled at. I suppose the tension between us was building for years and I just couldn't see it. My niece, Chelsea confided in me later that she needed new shoes and that they didn't have any money. I was overcome with self imposed guilt and responsibility. In the past I would have bought her the shoes and whatever else she wanted or needed. However, I now felt a financial obligation to my husband who had put us on a budget. I don't remember what exactly happened after that but I think it ended in an argument where Kristen became very angry with me and I tried to explain myself. On her behalf, no one asked me to buy Chelsea new shoes but I wanted her to have them. I felt it was my responsibility and I let it upset me. I probably could have bought her the new shoes but I felt it was a cycle I had created and I felt the pressure to break that cycle on behalf of my marriage. In hindsight, Kristen and Chelsea were always thankful for my munificence but I had set a precedent I could no longer maintain.

In 2002, also my first year of marriage, I came home without my husband because I had been evacuated from Cote d'Ivoire due to a terrible coup where more than 800 people were killed. My husband was required to stay to finish his assignment. It turned out that my dad had just suffered a heart attack and needed a triple bypass. I came home to help his wife Mame take care of him and bide my time until I could return to The Ivory Coast or my husband could join me back in the States. It was very special to be with my dad and Mame during this time. James and Kristen came over one night for dinner and they had plans to go out together afterward. They clearly didn't want me to come but I asked if I could anyway. They took me to a bar/liquor store. I really didn't know the two could be combined. It was fun watching them joking and laughing with their local friends and I was determined to show them I could be fun and that I didn't think I was superior to to them in any possible way. I knew this time I could show them my true heart. A man approached me and said, "Ma'm you're way too classy for this place, you don't belong here." It didn't hurt my feeling as if I wasn't welcomed. It bothered me because I wanted at that moment to fit in. I knew if a stranger walked up to me to say this, my brother and sister also knew I didn't belong there. I eventually talked them into going to a popular dance club on the beach. I danced with an old classmate who is so insignificant to this story I can't remember who he was. When it was time to leave, Kristen had disappeared with a man she had just met and it was just James and me. I'm guessing they went off to get some coffee somewhere quiet where they could talk. I had danced off any alcohol I'd consumed and I could see James was drunk. I asked him if I could drive home and he refused. He started driving us down a dirt road when I noticed him swerving and he couldn't stay in his lane. I asked him to please let me drive. He asked me why I ever bothered to come home and then he told me nobody wanted to see me, that my dad and Mame just tolerated me because they had to. Then he reached across me and flung open the passenger door of his truck. His eyes looked crazy and mean and I seriously thought he might hit me so I stepped out and stood there on the dark, dirt road and watched him drive away. No one had ever done anything like that to me before. I was terrified and could hardly process what had just happened. I could see the package store/bar where we had started the evening. I walked back as fast as I could terrified someone would pull over and yank me into their car. I was afraid to go back to my dad's house. I didn't know what my brother might do or say when I returned and I knew he would be there. How did I cover for my sister? I didn't want to make her look bad by telling my dad and Mame I didn't know where she was. I took a cab to the closest and unfortunately overpriced beach hotel and tried to sleep. The next morning I took a cab to my parents house. My brother had already told my dad that I was dirty dancing like a whore with some strange guy. I think my dad believed him because he looked suspicious and skeptical. For a few years following this event, I could see my dad's eyes following me, watching me, wondering if I was real or if I was a fraud. Jade had been my role model and I had learned so many of her ways whether I liked it or not. I also had similarities of Annie who had also betrayed my dad. I felt I was doomed to never truly win my dad's heart and I would never, ever win his trust. Jade told him terrible things about me growing up, Kristen thought I was a traitor, James called me a whore and Max later told my dad I did drugs and always played the martyr. In addition to all of this, my dad had been burned by women, two of them who I reminded him of. I reminded him of my birth mother in some ways and in other ways of Jade. How could I redeem myself? I resented the idea I had to.

CHAPTER 20-THE LAST TIME I SAW KRISTEN

Confabulation is that tendency for the brains of people who can't remember things to try to fill in the gaps of missing memory thereby making up an explanation that will answer questions.
This is particularly common among chronic alcoholics, though other brain issues also cause these symptoms.
It is common in chronic alcoholics, particularly those with Wernicke-Korsakoff's syndrome.
These two syndromes used to be listed separately but current usage is to consider them both parts of the same disorder.-*David Joel Miller, MS, Licensed Therapist & Licensed Counselor.*

The LAST time I saw Kristen was the worst. I had brought my boys who were 1 and 4 years old from Germany. I was also bringing two teenaged German sisters who lived across the street from us in Stuttgart, Germany. Their parents thought it would be a great opportunity for them to see the States and in return, they could help me with my children. My dad's wife, Mame co-owned a beach house with some family members and she suggested I rent it out so the boys could play on the beach. It was a reasonable price so I took her up on it. Kristen called me and said she wanted to come and stay with us. I couldn't wait to see her and my two nieces. Kristen showed up alone. She said she needed a break from her girls. I was disappointed at first but wanted to respect her needs. I thought we were having a good time yet I was tired from the overseas travel and caring for the boys. The teenage, German sisters were not helping me with the boys and I was becoming more and more exhausted. I felt so much pressure to entertain Kristen, the teenage girls and my own children. At one point I snapped at the girls and told them they had come to help me and they weren't carrying their weight. I felt like a monster, overridden with guilt and remorse for losing my temper. I just felt so weighed down with responsibility. I felt the same old familiar financial responsibility for my sister. She showed up with some alcohol but very little else. Here was another person to feed and entertain. I didn't see it as a burden. I saw it as a responsibility and I wanted my sister to have a good time.

One night during her visit, I went to sleep exhausted. I had traveled 21 hours with two small children and was still breastfeeding the youngest. I woke up the next morning and my sister was gone. We had scheduled a brunch with my dad's lovely wife, Mame and some other ladies and I was running out of time to get there. I couldn't find Kristen. She eventually returned my call to say that she had gone out to a beach bar, stayed the night somewhere else and was too hungover to come to brunch. I had to cover for her and it was awkward.

The next night was my last night in town and I just wanted to hang out and talk with my sister. We made dinner, I put the boys to bed and we just talked. She told me about the man she was currently dating. She said she loved him but she had a tendency of sabotaging healthy relationships. She told me her current boyfriend had a heart problem and she was afraid to commit because she was afraid something might happen to him. She was drinking heavily. Being a self acclaimed problem solver, I told her if she loved him, truly loved him, she should tell him and she should embrace this relationship heart problem or not because life is uncertain and "it is better to have loved and lost than to never have loved at all." We were sitting on the back steps of the beach house having what I thought was a meaningful conversation and listening to the Gulf of Mexico's waves rolling in and out. She bolted to her feet and suddenly said she needed to go. I thought I had helped inspire her to go declare her love for this man. Her house was one and a half hours away and she was slurring her words. It started pouring down rain like an omen and it took her several attempts to start her decrepit car. I begged her to stay yet she insisted on leaving. I packed all of the food from our trip in a cooler for her because we were flying back to Germany the next morning. I thought maybe she could use it and it could save her some money. I was so worried about her driving home in a faulty car, drunk and in the rain. She folded up a twenty dollar bill, leaned into me and carefully said, "I want you to have thissssss. For alllllllllllll that you have done and allll that youuuuuuuuuuuu have paid for......." I was so naive. I thought she was sincere.

I didn't want or need to take her money but I felt that I needed to respect her dignity and accept it, so I did.

Early the next morning, my niece and her daughter Chelsea called me crying hysterically. She said Kristen never showed to pick her and Lily up from their dad's house where they had stayed the few days Kristen had been visiting me. I didn't understand why it mattered so much until she explained. She said that their father (her step father) worked construction for time and a half pay on Saturdays and that Kristen had promised to pick them up in time for him to go to work. Chelsea was distraught and I could only picture Kristen dead in a ditch which would have been awful enough but to make it worse, I would have felt responsible. I prayed like I had never prayed before and tried to barter with God, "Let her be okay and I will do this or that or anything." I don't remember what it was I offered up in exchange for her safety. Then, reluctantly and out of desperation, I called Jade. Jade was always extremely resourceful and I knew she would know what to do. She and Kristen had been estranged for years and I didn't want to share Kristen's personal situation with her but I needed help. My dad and his sweet wife Mame would have been distraught and I couldn't tell them. Jade was the only mother I ever knew and I needed help. I needed a mom's help. I also wanted to believe that Jade loved Kristen and would help me find her. I don't know what Jade did, but she called me back and said that Kristen was not in jail or in the morgue. Shortly thereafter my niece Chelsea called sobbing again. She said they had found my sister Kristen passed out in her car. Apparently, she had made it home but just not inside her house. Chelsea was still crying and it wasn't a cry of relief. It was desperate and sad. That's when she said something I will never forget "Someone will go down for this, someone always does." In retrospect I know what she meant because her tone was a grieving goodbye to me. I thought she was concerned she would somehow be blamed and I assured her there was no way she could be blamed for this. I kept comforting her as she cried and I kept telling her she couldn't be blamed. She said I didn't understand. She was so right because I didn't know what lay in store for me.

When I returned to Africa, I needed to hear Kristen's voice. I had been so afraid she was killed in a car accident on her way home. I wanted to hear that she and her boyfriend were doing well and that she was okay. I needed to hear Chelsea wasn't in trouble. Once I finally spoke to Kristen, she was irate. She recounted our last evening together as if was completely different. She said I forced her to drive home in the rain and had been such a vain, snobby bitch she could no longer stand to be around me. She followed up with an email telling me that I was a horrible person, that she didn't like the way I treated people and that I "bad mouthed" the people that she loved. She literally wrote, "I don't like anything about you." She asked me to stay out of her life and to never contact her girls. I replied with carefully deliberate explanations but MOSTLY apologies. I was absolutely shocked and heartbroken when I never heard back. I decided to respect her wishes and that's what I did except for a couple of attempts to have her visit just to appease my dad. I knew the fact we were estranged hurt him deeply. The only other gesture I've made toward her was to send her all the cards she has ever given me along with some old pictures I thought she might appreciate. My message was meant to say, "Look! I have treasured you enough to keep and to carry these sentiments back and forth to Africa, to Europe and back to the States." I guess it was a last ditch effort to reconcile. It backfired because my niece, Nala (also her niece) reported that she was enraged by my gesture and was insulted by it. I told Nala why I was sending them and never understood why she didn't explain on my behalf when she had the chance. Didn't she want us to reconcile? I'm starting to see this desire for division bleed into the family's next generation and I have had to accept the loss of not only my siblings but my nieces and nephews as well.

CHAPTER 21-MARTYR

As we near the end, you can see by now, this story is not in sequential order and you will hear more about this story later. There was a time when my oldest brother Max had once said, "You're always the martyr." I started thinking about that a great deal. Was I? Was I really NOT treated that bad after all? Was I playing the martyr like I perceived Jade always did? I really soul searched. I wanted for so many years to be like Jade and for so many years not to be nothing like her. I revisited the times she was sick whenever my dad had a fishing trip and she guilted him. I remembered how she would lay in the bed so sick as he left, read books all day and then when he came home from fishing guilt him for leaving her sick and alone. I remembered all the times she told me her doctors thought she had this or that horrible disease. Was she a hypochondriac?

I can absolutely never forget when I was maybe
ten years old, she told me that her doctors
thought she had leukemia and my dad just so
happened to be away fishing. Other times she
said her doctors thought she was a hemophiliac
or was having a stroke. There always seemed to
be something wrong with her. Eventually, I
stopped reacting. It wasn't that I didn't believe
her or that I didn't care. It was that her
symptoms and illnesses just became the norm.
One might think it should almost be comical
now that I'm informed and no longer ignorant. I
know now what leukemia looks like, I know she
probably didn't have all of these diagnoses so I
should laugh but that's not how I feel. She had a
sickness much deeper than anything she ever
fabricated. I believe she was/is possibly
mentally ill. Growing up with a dramatic
mother who fabricated illnesses, I can see how
Max may have thought I was dramatizing the
way she treated me. He may have also
subconsciously felt guilty about the familial
divide between the hads and the had-nots.

Decades later when I lived in Africa for the second time and my boys were two and five years old, Jade called to tell me she had breast cancer. I felt like a daughter whose mother had breast cancer.

My husband's job as Military Attache' to the embassy came with a palatial house and every room had a balcony, most of which had never been accessed. I didn't want my toddlers to see how upset I was so I went to a random guest room and sat on the dirty balcony and solemnly cried for her. I remember cobwebs, lizards and insects making their way across this balcony as I cried. I felt as if I was invading their territory and I didn't belong.

I wanted to go home and take care of my one and only mom, Jade. I called her and asked if I could come and take care of her. We had several nannies in Africa that could care for my children and I wanted more than anything to come home and care for her. I was delusional to think she considered me her daughter. When I begged to come take care of her, she used these exact cutting words "Well, right now, I'm not up for any visitors." I didn't want to be a visitor; I wanted to be a daughter. She had a Caring-bridge account online. She posted ad nauseum how much her daughter Demi had been there for her during this unfathomable journey. I was so happy Demi had been there for her but I so desperately wanted to have been there for her too as her daughter. It was painfully obvious that to Jade I wasn't her daughter. Instead I was JUST another visitor and this cut deeply into my heart. I was confronted with the fact I was considered a cumbersome visitor while Demi was considered her angel. I was willing to leave my tiny toddlers in the care of nannies who didn't even speak English to come take care of who I thought was my mother. I was starting to get tired of getting kicked away when I was only begging for one small bone. I was beginning to not need those bones anymore.

A year or two later, I was having some health problems of my own. There wasn't a hospital in Mozambique where my husband was serving as the Military Attache'. Whenever we had even a doctor's appointment, we had to fly to Pretoria, South Africa. I needed what's considered a major surgery in Pretoria. This is where I painfully longed for a mother. I missed my children and had to stay in Pretoria for weeks following my surgery for recovery and follow up. I emailed my mom, Jade a long heart-felt letter. I told her I wanted to set her free of me. I wrote that I felt I had been pushing myself on her since the divorce and I realized it might be easier for her if I left her alone. I explained I was looking for more than I thought she was willing to give and it was okay for her to live her life without me as long as she was happy. I believed and I do believe right here, right now that if we love someone and they are happier without us in their life, we should let them be. I have learned to do that with Kristen, James, Max, and Demi. They may have been more important to me than I was to them and it makes perfect sense psychologically. They have had more life without me during their formidable years. I wanted to set Jade free of me too but instead of interpreting my letter the way I intended it, she wrote me back a hateful email. The only specific thing I remember her saying was that she would put it in the file with all of the other nasty letters I have written her over the years.

I don't remember writing her any mean letters over the years but apparently, she has them filed away for whatever reason. I don't get it.

CHAPTER 22- THE MARVELOUS MRS MAME & 9/11

Let them judge you.
Let them misunderstand you.
Let them gossip about you.
Their opinions aren't your problem.
You stay kind, committed to love,
and free in your authenticity.
No matter what they do or say,
don't you dare doubt your worth
or the beauty of your truth.
Just keep on shining like you do."
— *Scott Stabile*

I talked to my dad's wife, Mame about it and I learned so much from this woman I had formerly and wrongfully dismissed as maybe just a tad naive. She was much wiser than I had ever imagined. She taught me about jealousy and about alcoholism without saying anything derogatory about anyone, not even Jade.

She said every time my name was mentioned that certain people would stiffen, their faces would harden and blinding jealousy would spark from their eyes. She suggested they were perhaps jealous my dad was proud of me. I gave up a very successful career to marry a man who would become a Colonel in the Army and live abroad as a diplomat. I had a nice home, a nice life, and two sweet boys. I also had these children with my husband in wedlock, unlike others. This doesn't matter so much to me in regard to others but we all know that it does to my dad.

I didn't have any debt and didn't give my dad any real reason to worry about me. I felt guilty anyone would be jealous of me and I wondered how I could have changed that. I thought about beautiful, successful people I know who don't seem to have these type of problems. Why did I? Mame said that I had just made different and better choices than others and I felt guilty for that too.

I thought about the psychologist who told me that Kristen and James could have suffered more greatly and differently than I had because they were older when they lost their mother. She explained how the damage might have been greater. I also knew that Kristen and James probably thought that I received special privileges from Jade like Demi and Max had. I had heard they thought I kept a relationship with her after the divorce not only because I was a traitor but for monetary reasons as well. They thought because my life seemed easier, it must have been because I was granted something extra along the way; something they had been denied. Also, they were at the time, both alcoholics and didn't remember things clearly. Mame told me when alcoholics don't remember details, they make them up. She said alcoholics fill the voids they don't remember with fabrications that work to their advantage.

This is what Chelsea meant on the phone when they found Kristen passed out in her car after driving home drunk in the rain. "Someone's going down for this, someone always does." It suddenly made sense. Chelsea knew I would be the one who would be blamed for this and she was going to miss me. And oh, how I have consequently missed her all of these years.

Kristen was a teenager when my dad and Jade married. She had already forged her own entry into womanhood with no role model. She had suffered the loss of a memorable mother. She had felt the burden of caring for two younger siblings and a lonely dad. Her burden was so different from mine. How could I judge her for anything? I know she would never want to be pitied. I don't pity her. I wish things had been different for her growing up and I wish that I had known how to be there for her. I have a distant, residual admiration for her. I remember the times she made me laugh, I think she's been a good mother to her girls and despite her feelings toward me, I think she's inherently a good person. I just think she is so deeply hurting inside that she needs to project that hurt elsewhere. I think because I am physically out of sight and out of mind, I make a good depository.

I'm reminded of my family every 9/11. Different news programs interview families who lost loved ones that tragic day and they all say how much those people are missed. It hits me in the strangest place. These people would do anything to see their loved ones again. For years, I felt sad that my siblings and "mom" wouldn't miss me at all. They haven't missed all these years I've been right here waiting for them to remember me. The truth is I don't think James loves me. As a matter of fact, Nala told me that he refers to me as the "half-sister" and with disgust. She said when she told my dad, he confessed that it was true but that he hadn't known. It's interesting that my dad won't discuss it with me and it's interesting that Nala said he was very upset to hear James refer to me as "the half-sister." I don't know why I could hardly believe my ears to hear that he said that. I don't believe that Max loves me either, or Demi. I choose to go ahead and believe that Kristen must have some love in there somewhere left for me but I'm starting to wonder if it even matters anymore. My life is now full of friends and my own family, my own children who treasure me, would defend me to the end of the earth and miss me terribly if I were gone.

"People, even more than things, have to be restored, renewed, revived, reclaimed, and redeemed; never throw out anyone." — *Audrey Hepburn*

Mame says it's never too late but I feel it is. I was discarded by all four of my brothers and sisters too long ago as if I meant nothing to them at all.

I confessed to a therapist "Four out of four of my brothers and sister despise me. How can I possibly deny that it's my fault? Statistically it's obvious that it has to be." We talked for hours and hours and for thousands of dollars to boot. She said sometimes after our sessions she felt the need to open a window to let out the grief and the pain that filled the air. She said sometimes after our sessions she cried. Other times, she thought about my family and wished she could help each one of them. I did too. This therapist asked me a great deal of questions about each person that discarded me. She was actually able to explain why it wasn't all of my fault. She said Jade was a seriously disturbed person.

She helped me understand the way Jade spun webs of deception and drove wedges between my siblings and me and between my father and me, James and my father and so on. I began to imagine her as a black spider with green eyes. This was twenty years ago and I began writing journal entries about a spider that spun webs and caught each of us and delighted in our demise. She really did just that. Why? Why? Why? That mattered so much for so many years but it just doesn't anymore.

BECAUSE: I l believe with all my heart (and my children and husband will attest this is my motto)

It's so much easier to pass judgement than to seek understanding- Me

All this time, I thought I was quoting a bible verse or a famous quote. However, when I went to find it online, I found a ton of quotes and bible verses similar but not these exact words………….hmmmmmmm.

CHAPTER 23-FANTASIES & EDUCATION

I fantasized my siblings will one day finally see my honest heart, who I am and understand how much residual love I have for them. They were all older than me when we became a family. I never saw a difference in step siblings and half sibling but they understandably did. I honestly and easily loved them all equally. I think it was easier for me because I had little memory before Jade and my dad married. They did. It doesn't bother me that they meant more to me than I may have meant to them. It makes sense psychologically.

On my behalf, I have seen many therapists over the years who have consistently concurred that I make sense and I am able to see into the human condition. I'm able to understand things in a way many people can't. I don't necessarily take pride in this. I take comfort in it. I sometimes feel like a self proclaimed psychologist. However, I would never, ever, subject myself to going back to college for a real degree, not after the agony of the first round where I flunked out and dropped classes left and right. I know if I did, I would succeed this time. I just really don't want to.

I'm glad that times have changed and that schools now evaluate students for learning challenges and provide IEPs and 504s. I understand now why everyone doesn't go to college. Some of our parents weren't attentive to our educations for whatever reason. Some of us worked and went to school and couldn't balance it all, especially without any guidance.

I do believe however, it's a parents duty to guide their children. It's the parent who should make sure the child does their homework and gets it turned in on time, to make sure they are well fed before school and even guide them through the social aspects that go getting along in school. I would never think of doing any less for my children, and I have advocated for them endlessly to get them what they need and deserve. No one did this for James, Kristen, me or so many other people out there in the world. It's hard for privileged people or those who come from academically centered families to understand this. Seeking this understanding could be one small step in bringing our nation closer together as a whole.

CHAPTER 24- THERAPY & JADE REFLECTIONS

I went to a counselor a few years back, mainly for my current and normal family challenges. He was the only provider in my area who accepted my insurance. I would go on and on and he never really said much in return. Eventually, it seemed I would catch him checking his email and texting as I poured out my heart. He would dig the wax out of his ears and wipe it on his jeans while he seemed to be pondering something deep. I found these habits disgusting and I didn't know how much longer I could tolerate it. Sometimes, he almost looked like he was falling asleep.

Finally, one day I snapped and said, "Well?! What do you think?! Don't you have an opinion, advice, anything to offer up?!"

He said, "No, Kathryn, you don't need my opinion, you already know what you need to know. You just need to hear yourself say the words."

I confronted him about his texting while I was confiding my thoughts and secrets. He told me he wasn't texting, that he was taking notes. He told me I was giving HIM insight and giving him thoughts and ideas that he needed to ponder and could possibly help other patients. He told me I was one of the most emotionally intelligent people that he had ever met. "Wow, I thought, I'll take that, ear wax and all!" This is why early on, Jade knew that I "had her number." I saw through things others couldn't. As afraid as I was of her, I wish I understood how afraid she was of me. Although I was tenacious to win her love, I had insight into her web spinning ways. She knew she had to alienate me, to sabotage my relationships and to discredit me. She spent decades doing this. Meanwhile, I was a stray dog. I came to her back door day after day begging for scraps. Some days I would be kicked and scared away. Other days, I would get a scrap or a bone. This kept me, the desperate and hungry dog coming back for more day after day, year after year, and decade after decade. When you're desperate and starving, you get accustomed to being kicked away because you know that maybe, just maybe there are some days where you'll get thrown a bone.

CHAPTER 24- REWIND & WEDGES

After the divorce, I always expected that Max or
Demi would come and visit me at Jade's house
when I came to town but they never, ever did.
Not once. I found that a little odd but never
asked why. Deep down I knew that it was
because of the wedge Jade had strategically put
between us.

The starving dog and the psychologist in me
started noticing and collecting data from day
one.

It's ironic though, that I didn't notice certain
things because at times I was also that frog
slowly boiling to death in the pot or I was the
flounder just trying to blend in and get by. I was
the desperately hungry dog hoping for a bone
or I was the step daughter that on occasion
might do something to make her vain
stepmother proud.

These are the times I remember making her proud: Winning a Bible Bowl. I studied so hard that I answered every single question; not a single student on my team had the chance to even try to answer a question and I came home with the team trophy. Once, when I was in high school, Jade and I were driving and some men in the car to the right of us started trying to get my attention. They were in an expensive car and she was tickled that they found me attractive. She told me I shouldn't waste my time going to college. She said I needed to use my looks to marry a doctor. I thought back to the times she said I had buck teeth and I had strange yellow eyes. I remember when I was little, she told me that people only told me I was cute out of pity. Yes, of course, I mention being told I was decent looking in appearance multiple times in this story. The irony, is I couldn't see it. I looked in the mirror and saw an ugly bastard in the same way an anorexic sees a fat girl when she looks in the mirror.

Jade taught me that love was conditional for me. It was always performance based. Not only did I never forget she told me I was lucky to have a roof over my head and she and my dad owed me nothing, I believed it. It became the root of my actions for many, many years to come. It became the premise to every decision I made. I was on my own and I was alone in the world. I held multiple jobs at a time. I ate nothing but Taco Bell 69 cent bean burritos for weeks at a time. At one point, I rented a cheap room in a house with a bunch of other girls near the campus of the University of Alabama. The only room available was tiny and in the back of the house.

The house was covered in roaches and some of the other girls had what I thought were nasty, unsanitary habits. One stole the few clothes I had and I would find them wadded up and soiled in the garbage. There was a night when I was sleeping on my back and I had a weird feeling that someone was watching me. The street light was shining through the window so I looked around for an intruder in the same way I laid frozen in my bed when I was a child waiting for the monster to jump out from underneath my bed. I saw something twitching and looked down on my chest to find an enormous cockroach staring me in the face. At the time, I was briefly dating the son of a prominent college basketball coach and he was able to provide Jade and my dad fifty yard line tickets to the Alabama/Auburn game, (a very big deal down south.) Jade was proud of me for that brief moment. My desire for her acceptance over road my subconscious truth. I wanted to be accepted for who I was, the good, the bad and the ugly. I wanted her to notice I was living in filth, not because I wanted to but because I was in such a bad place financially. I needed help but wouldn't ask for it. My dad was oblivious and she wouldn't help me flounder my way out of this water. Now that I'm a mother of teenagers, I can see what she could have done if you truly cared about me. She could have asked questions, she could have brought me home, she could have moved me out and found me a better place to live. Instead, she went to the Alabama game, stayed in a nice hotel and went home.

I watched my sorority friends go off to boutique gyms for aerobic classes and they brought me along as a guest on a few occasions. I wanted a membership so badly. I couldn't afford it but I had an idea. Aerobics looked a lot like cheerleading moves that were repeated over and over to music. I knew I was coordinated and had cheered for many years so I applied for jobs as an aerobic instructor and I got them. I played random music I liked and directed the students to do whatever came to my mind. It worked! I became friends with more and more sorority girls through teaching aerobics and they included me in their outings and parties when I wasn't working. However, I worked all the time. I taught aerobics at 6am, went to class from 8am to 12pm and worked from 12-9pm at a department store. I had to leave class early to get to work, and try to do my homework during my lunch hour. I rarely did homework when I came home; instead I went out with my friends. Something had to suffer and I admit that most of the time it was my grades. I dropped classes when I remembered to do so and other times just stopped going to class and took an F. I had literally no idea what my future held and no long term guidance. My sorority friends went on beach vacations and cruises over spring break while I picked up extra hours at work.

Never once did I feel sorry for myself because this was my normal. I didn't expect to ever be able to do those things so I thoroughly enjoyed their stories about what seemed like exotic trips to me.

I finally decided I'd had enough of college and applied for a flight attendant position with Southwest Airlines. There were hundreds of girls at the first interview and I didn't think I stood a change. They told us up front that they were going to choose about 10% of us. I knew I wouldn't make it but I thought the interview process would be a fun experience. I was called back for a second interview and to my surprise a third and final interview. The final interview was in Atlanta and by this point I had transferred to University of South Alabama and was living in Mobile. I drove up the night before the interview and had planned to stay with a dear high school friend who lived there named Susie. Right outside of Atlanta, I hit something on the dark road. The next thing that I knew, all four tires of my car were flat. Terrified, I found my way to a pay phone. I didn't have a credit card and I had very little cash. Dreadfully, I had no choice but to call Jade and my dad for help. Jade answered the phone and when I told her I needed help, she cupped her hand over the phone and I could hear her whining pitifully to my dad. The next voice I heard was my dad's on the phone and he was furious with me. He said, "How dare you call us up at night when we are already in bed asking for money. No! Your mom is sick and we can't help you this time." He hung up the phone and I stood there in the phone booth with the words "this time" ringing through my head. I had never asked for help before and I was stranded all alone outside of Atlanta in a phone booth. I remembered a guy that I had gone on a few dates with before who lived in Atlanta. He had already graduated and had a good job. Reluctantly, I called him. He came and picked me up, paid for my tires and let me sleep in his bed while he took the couch. The next morning, when I woke up, he had gone to work. I left him a thank you note, went to my interview and was given the job. For decades, I wanted to thank him but I could no longer find him. When things were going really well for me financially, I tried to find him not only to pay him back but to surprise him with some extravagant gift but I couldn't find a single person with his same name. Even with Facebook now, no one with that name even exists.

My flight attendant training wasn't to begin for another six months so I worked multiple jobs and saved up to cover car payments and have spending money while I was in training. It was during this time that I met and fell in love with the beautiful Jeff in Mobile. We were completely crazy about each other and he planned to meet me in Texas where and when I would complete my six month training. Jade was proud of me momentarily when I was accepted into the Southwest Flight attendant program. Those are literally the only memories I have of her being proud of me and all of these were so shallow. That's what made me sad. On one visit home, after having worked hard to reach an executive level position in a previous job, Jade said, "I have to say that in spite of me, you have made something of yourself." That day, I thought I felt the heavens open up, that she was finally truly proud of me for something worthwhile and that she was taking responsibility for her faults. I was wrong. She was playing games with me again. For whatever reason, she was unwinding her thread and letting me think I was going free, just to spin her threads tightly back around me soon after.

Backing up a little: I was living in Dallas and had become dear friends with my oldest brother Max and his wife Jessica#2 as a young adult in my twenties. It felt so fantastic to be friends with my oldest brother as an adult. He and his second wife had an enormous house and he had moved out of broadcasting and into banking. They were doing very well. Jessica#2 and I became almost like best friends. I thought it was the coolest thing in the world to go over to my brothers house, cook out and drink beer with my brother ten years older than me! Eventually I learned that Max and Jessica#2 were recreationally experimenting with marijuana and cocaine. My inconsequential boyfriend at the time and I went over to their house for a small party. I definitely did try both marijuana and cocaine with them. I didn't like the pot and I didn't do enough of the cocaine to feel anything. It was really just an act. This was shortly after the divorce and Max and Jessica#2 were upset with Jade. We told some of their friends at the party what Jade had done to my dad. They were all high everyone except my boyfriend and me. They decided to prank call Jade and I don't remember exactly what they said but it was very ugly and I felt really uncomfortable. I had this residual fear of her, that she would know somehow I was there. I asked my boyfriend if we could leave and we did. I knew Jade was very resourceful and seemed somehow to know things that couldn't be explained. I felt for sure she would trace the call or somehow figure it out and I didn't want any part of it. I also didn't want to be part of hurting her or anyone else.

Weeks later, Max's wife and my sister in law, Jessica#2 told me she thought I was one of the prettiest women she had ever known. This was shocking to hear. Then again, every compliment on my appearance was shocking as if it were the first time I had heard it. I often thought it was a trick or someone must have wanted something from me. Jade had taught me this when I was only sixteen when I received some anonymous roses from a boy that wanted to meet me. When I excitedly brought the roses home, Jade told me, "If it seems too good to be true, it probably is." She disapproved of the roses and forbid me to meet the boy. I then saw him as someone dirty and wrong and I allowed her to rob me of this joy. So, when Jessica#2 followed her compliment with "Max disagrees and said that he doesn't think you are pretty at all" it seemed normal. "She must have some skewed view of what 'pretty' is," I thought. She said she was relieved to hear him say this because she had been feeling uncomfortable about our adult friendship and how close Max and I were becoming. I told her that he was my brother and asked her what was there to be jealous of. She said she was afraid he would be sexually attracted to me because we weren't real siblings. I didn't really mind that he didn't think I was pretty. What really, really hurt was the thought of him not being my brother. I never thought about that. I always thought of all four of my siblings as my siblings. Although, this story requires me to make the differentials to make it digestible, I never thought or said anyone was my step brother or my half brother or sister.

I didn't think about it in the same way that I didn't think about Jade not being my real mother. I had almost brainwashed myself so when people mentioned the facts of us not being blood related, it hurt. It hurt because to me, and only me, it didn't matter. I believe it was no coincidence that after this conversation, Jessica #2, my brother, Max and my relationships began to unravel.

Jessica#2 started finding reasons to avoid me. Max's children from his first marriage to the original Jessica came to visit from out of town and I wanted to see them. I took a vacation day from work so that we could all go to an amusement park. Jessica#2 had made all of the plans for us. I called the morning of to ask what time I should meet them. I don't remember all of the details but I do remember that Max was very rude and told me I was no longer invited. I was really sad but I notoriously didn't ask any questions.

Months later, my dad told me he was coming to Dallas for Thanksgiving and that I should meet him, Max and Jessica#2 at a lake house about an hour out of town. I asked Jessica#2 what I should bring and she told me to bring just a bag of chips. I was on a very tight budget at the time and I think she just wanted me to make a minimal contribution based on the gesture.

I worked late the night before Thanksgiving. By this time, I was engaged to a very sweet young man. I remember this trip to the lake house was really inconvenient for us but we went regardless because it was Thanksgiving and I wanted to see my dad. I think it was because we were rushing to coordinate to get there, we forgot the chips. I offered to run out and get some but Jessica#2 told me it wasn't a big deal.

Jessica#2 and I were the only two women at the lake house and she was distant and wouldn't engage in my attempts at conversation. She sat on the balcony smoking cigarettes and if I tried to talk to her she curled her lips up in a little smirk, looked away and shook her head like people do when they can't be bothered. She expected me to know what was wrong yet I had no idea. Now that I am much older and much more confident, I wouldn't hesitate to confront her and to ask if I had done something to upset or offend her. Back then, I couldn't do it. In hindsight, I think she was high or on prescription drugs. I knew she took a lot of prescription drugs for a back problem but I think it may have gotten out of hand as we know from the opioid crisis that it often does. I had been prescribed some pain killers years earlier after a sinus surgery. I knew that she had taken my painkillers when she came to visit me. I knew she had gone to the pharmacy to get my refill and kept it for herself. I had not judged her because she had serious back pain and I didn't want the pain killers anyway.

When you're as insecure as I was, you don't think about the fact that someone else could possibly be the one with the problem. I thought that if she was jealous of me, it must be because of something I had done. I believed wholeheartedly if she was ignoring me and acting strange it was entirely my fault. The men were inside talking about sports and fishing and I wanted my new fiancé to bond with them so I let it be. Jessica#2 had prepared and/or purchased the entire Thanksgiving meal but after the meal was over she didn't pick up a single plate to clean up. The men went back to the living room and I washed every single pot, pan and dish. I assumed it was the trade off because she had prepared the meal before I was able to arrive but it was still odd. Later that day, I was walking through the living room when I ran into a stretched out fishing line. Max began screaming at me. He said they had been restringing a fly fishing line and that I had just ruined it. I looked up and that's exactly what they were doing. I just didn't see it. I apologized but he kept yelling.

He yelled at me for not being alert, for forgetting the chips, for not helping Jessica #2 prepare the meal. He flung in random things and some legitimate mistakes I had made in the past. For example, I had received some money from my insurance company for a fender bender. Instead of getting my car fixed, I used it to pay my rent. He yelled at me for that. Once I applied for a job at the corporate fitness center at the company where he worked. On my application, I wrote that I had attended University of Alabama instead of University of South Alabama. I don't know why. I honestly don't. It wasn't a blatant lie where I fabricated this information. I just left out the word "south." However, when the company called University of Alabama, there were naturally no transcripts for me. My brother said that this was incredibly embarrassing for him and I understood that. However, he had unbeknownst to me been harboring this resentment for years. He had never, ever mentioned it before. I had no idea until this outburst. I could see that Jessica#2 had been fueling this fire in the same way that Jade had always done to my dad. She had been fueling his fire since the day she told me that she was jealous because we were only step brother and sister. The day she gave me the backhanded compliment that she thought I was gorgeous but then made sure I knew that he didn't find me attractive. I had never cared if either of my brothers thought I was pretty or not; ewh. My dad was watching Max's verbal attack on me. My then fiancé' (with whom I never married) and I tried to leave. Instead of coming to my defense, my dad came out to the car, grabbed me by my throat and pressed me into the car seat where I couldn't breathe. With his teeth clenched, he told me I needed to get my shit together. My fiancé' talked him into letting go. My dad later apologized to me with tears streaming down his face. He said he was going through a very hard time getting over Jade. He said I had said or done something in response to Max that reminded him of her and he just snapped. It took me years to get over this but I don't even think about it anymore. It's been more than twenty years ago and the last time my dad ever lost his temper with me. That version of him has faded away with his feelings for Jade. Like a drug addiction, she was the poison that was still in his system at the time.

At this point, I was on speaking terms with Jade and Demi. I came to Panama City to visit. My stomach was always in knots trying to balance my time between my dad and Jade. I felt guilty when I went to see Jade and guilty when I didn't. Coincidentally, I still occasionally dream I am conflicted and stressed about visiting Jade and I wake up feeling very unsettled. Jade and I went over to see Demi for a short dutiful visit. I couldn't believe my eyes when I walked through the door. It's funny now because she had never visited me and she stood proudly as if I was amazed with her home and decor. Little did she know, I didn't necessarily care for her style yet I had a lucrative job and had a beautiful condo I was equally as proud of. If my jaw dropped at the sight of her home, this is why. Demi's house was full of my mom's furniture; really nice furniture. She also had her grandfather clock, expensive art and knick knacks that I recognized from Jade's home. She was wearing some expensive jewelry that had belonged to Jade. Demi sized me up with her eyes. We were both very fit at the time and I could see her noticing everything, my body, my hair, my clothes yet she wasn't listening to a single word I said. That was until Jade and Demi asked me about my relationship with Jessica#2 and Max. Regretfully, I said we had become very good friends in Dallas, we had talked frequently and that I often visited their house. Demi became very angry and she said these exact words "I can't believe he has YOU 'all up' in his house, yet he can't even ever call his REAL sister!" To hear someone say it out loud was heart wrenching for me. What did she mean? Nooooooo. To hear her say that they really didn't consider me their sister sent my heart tumbling down the hill with Jack and Jill. And when it hit the bottom, it was left with bruises that lasted for years to come. I wanted to flounder deep into the sand where no one could see me. I felt so alone in the world, again.

Because Jessica#2 had become mysteriously skinny, they asked me if I thought she took prescription drugs. All I wanted in the world at that moment was for Jade and Demi to love me. I felt desperate. I told them I knew she did. Then they asked me if she and Max did recreational drugs and I said, "Yes" again. They asked me if I knew anything about the prank call and I said a final and fatal "yes." At the time, I blamed Jessica#2 and Max for my dad almost strangling me and I didn't care at that moment about how making this confession would affect them. I didn't do it spitefully to hurt Max and JESSICA#2. I did it desperately for Demi and Jade and I really believed I was only confirming a secret they already knew. Little did I know they would use it to destroy my relationship with Max and Jessica#2. Little did I know just how little I really mattered to any of them. Jade and Demi didn't hesitate to throw me under the bus. Just like Demi not wanting me to have a parakeet when I was a little girl, she also didn't want me to have a friendship with my brother Max. Jade would see to it I didn't.

When we returned to Jade's house, I gathered up my courage and asked her if she had anything belonged to her that she didn't mind me having. I wanted something that represented her. It was my last ditch effort to try and feel like a daughter; I wanted to feel like Demi. I needed to fill the hole that Demi had just dug out of my heart by reminding me I wasn't a real sister and AND I also wasn't a real daughter. I thought if Jade gave me something that belonged to her, just one thing, it would prove that I somehow mattered. She went over to one of several china cabinets and dug around in the back bottom shelf. The bottom shelf, the back of the bottom shelf. The shelf where people keep things they never use, the shelf where you might dig something out for a garage sale. She dug out a cheap glass compote I had seen her serve banana pudding in on occasion and said, "I guess you can have this." I remember the look on her face. It was somewhere in between indifference and being slightly put out. I temporarily bounced back into "happy" and moved on.

CHAPTER 25-APERTURE

"The first time someone shows you who they are, believe them." -- *Maya Angelou*

Jade told me a story about her daschund that had been just been attacked by a neighbor's dog. As I watched and listened, I felt like I was seeing someone different for the first time. As if seeing her through an aperture, she no longer looked refined and tasteful. She didn't look beautiful anymore either. It wasn't due to aging. I think beautiful, elegant women stay that way for their lifetime. I know many women in their 70's and 80's who still exude beauty and class. What was different about Jade? Had she let herself go? No, that wasn't it. Her story about the dog attack seemed embellished and tragic but when I looked over at the dachshund, I didn't see a scrape or even a single hair out of place. She turned the word "attacked" into a two syllable word "attack-ed." At first, I thought it was a slip of the tongue until she continued to pronounce it that way over and over again.

I suddenly noticed her floppy hair style and I hated it. I remembered her hair always being perfectly coiffed.

The phone rang and instead of taking it in the other room like she did when Demi or Jessica#2 called, she came back into the room and paced dramatically, demanding my attention as if trying to solve a monstrous problem. At least I knew this time she wasn't whispering about me. This was different; she wanted me to hear every word of this conversation. She hurried to her hand bag and took out her credit card. She told the person not to worry and that she would take care of it right away. She asked the person for her birth date and hung up the phone. With a self induced breathlessness, she explained that someone from her church needed a plane ticket to leave her dangerous husband and she was called upon to purchase it.

Jade elaborated that everyone at the new church she and Wyatt attended came to her with their problems. She was bragging! She said she was constantly bailing people out of their problems and that she and Wyatt were revered as leaders of the church. Maybe she thought this role at her new church counter-balanced the fact that she and Wyatt had been ostracized from the church they had belonged to since I was five years old. This is the church where my dad belongs and I will always consider my home. After their affair was discovered, they were no longer felt welcome at the church they had attended for decades. Notice I didn't say, "They were made to feel unwelcome by the church." My guess is that the infidelity by itself gave them the impression they would no longer be welcome. With love and compassion, I hope that it brings them both some peace to feel valued at their current church. No one should have to carry a cross for their mistakes for the rest of their lives and I'm not judging her decision to leave my dad and marry Wyatt. That's why Kristen and James find me so repulsive. Although, I have let Jade go, I still don't harbor resentment for what she did to my dad. Mostly because it allowed him to find Mame; also because the lyrics to this song have explained it to me for decades.

Here is just one line:

There ain't no good guy, there ain't no bad guy
There's only you and me and we just disagree-
Dave Mason

Watching her pacing as she spoke on the phone with the church member reminded me of the time in my twenties when she told everyone at church that I had precancerous cells from having too much sex and she had to rush to my rescue. I wondered if she told this lie with the same theatrics. In love and compassion, I wonder if she was just truly ignorant about what causes precancerous cells. Regardless, she didn't need to share such information. As she continued her performance, I started thinking of other times; many other times when she made things out to be more than they were. I thought about the way she whispered on the phone to Demi when I came to visit yet Demi never came over to see me. The same with Jessica#2! What was she telling them about me after all? True, she could have been whispering to them about something private that had nothing to do with me, but she wasn't it and I knew it. And I had known it all along. I just didn't want to see it. This is when the clouds in my mind, my heart and my soul started to part. It would still be a while before it was a cloudless day but in hindsight, it was coming.

Jade and I usually made a token trip to the mall when I visited and she would buy me some random thing; one thing. I allowed this gesture to make me feel indebted to her. On our way home on this particular visit, she wanted to stop at a drive through Sonic to get something to eat. Sonic was a place I had only been to once or twice many years ago for an "slush." The only thing I could eat on the menu was french fries because I am a vegetarian. She ordered some weird looking chili dog and we sat there and ate in the car. I'm in no way above eating at Sonic but this seemed odd to me. I had never seen Jade eat a hot dog and especially not in the car. It seemed gross and wrong because I had remembered her never allowing food in her car as if it was beneath her. This didn't match my image of her. As we sat there quietly eating, I wondered why she had referred to my "yellow eyes" as if they were a disgrace. Why did she always tell me I had buck teeth? I wondered why she had provoked my dad to beat James and me when we were little. I wondered why she did so much for random people from her church but so little for me. I wondered so many things. I asked her "Mom, was your mother nice to you?" She began to rave about her mother and how much she loved her. I asked her "Did something bad happen to you when you were a child or a young woman?" She looked at me like I had asked her something ridiculous. She said, "No?" with a question inflection as if she was daring me to go on. I wanted to know; I needed to know. Why did she treat us this way? Why did she try to ruin Kristen and James' lives? I felt like I was seeing her for the first time. I was still somewhat happy that she spared me the cheap glass banana pudding compote when I packed it up in my luggage and went back to wherever it was that I lived during this particular visit. I don't remember how long it was after I put it in a cabinet in my home but one random day, I opened the cabinet and saw that stupid compote for what it really was and what it represented. I noticed a seam where the glass had been fused down one side and I thought about how much I hated banana pudding. I hated when the vanilla wafers became soggy and the bananas started to turn brown. I took the compote out and gently tossed it in the garbage can. No anger, no contempt, no sadness, nothing.

By this point, my dad had already married The Marvelous Mame and we were scheduled to meet her grown children and grandchildren at her family beach house. I was still getting to know Mame and was happy to go. I was also so happy my dad had finally found a good woman.

We were all settling in when Max and Jessica arrived. I had forgotten about my confession to Demi and Jade. I wasn't concerned about it because I thought it was something they already knew but stupidly and most importantly, I trusted them that it wouldn't go anywhere. Max huffed through the door without saying anything to anyone. He charged straight toward me and in a most condescending way said, "We need to talk. Go to the bedroom!" In hindsight, there was Jessica#2 in the peripheral and in just the way Jade had always fueled my dad's rage. Jade had also started this fire yet with Jessica#2 as the catalyst, they had created an explosion. In a daze, I went to the bedroom feeling nothing, frozen really. He towered over me and jabbed his finger into my collar bone shouting at me again. I was completely overwhelmed with surprise. He said his ex-wife and mother of his children didn't want him to visit his own children because I told her that he and Jessica#2 took drugs. With Mame's entire family outside the open door, he said that I was the one who did drugs and that I was the one who made the prank phone call, that I dialed the number and had spoken. Jessica#2 backed him up. They were convincing. So believable that for a second, I questioned myself.

Gas lighting.

But I knew that I didn't. I remember that I
didn't even know Jade's new phone number at
the time. I also remember thinking I could never
get away with a prank call because I am
notorious for my high pitched nasal voice. I
hated my voice almost as much as I hated my
yellow eyes and buck teeth. I have never been
able to disguise my voice and I would never
dare. I also reflected on how afraid I was when
they made those calls.
I had this remnant fear that Jade could do
anything. She could trace the calls or had some
kind of telepathic powers. I KNEW I didn't do
it. At the time and more many years, I believed
my confession greatly affected Max's
relationship with his ex wife and children. With
love and compassion, I understand him being
upset if he believed this would cost him the
trust of his children. However, I don't think he
considered the compromised position that I had
found myself in with Demi and Jade. Of course
I regretted telling them. Giving this confession
to Jade and Demi didn't salvage my relationship
with them, it just isolated me from Max and
Jessica#2 and destroyed our relationship.

I believe that they remember the drug incident differently than I do and that over time, they have convinced themselves it happened another way. How can I redeem myself when their memory has become their truth? The only way would be to confess something that wasn't my truth. And out of the self love and respect I have worked so hard to be able to extend to myself, I wouldn't do it. Also, I learned recently from Jessica#1, Max's first wife, (the homecoming queen) that Jade and Demi never told her about the drug incident and that it had not affected Max's relationship at all. She never even knew about it at all.

On another visit, Mame told me that Max and Jessica#2 wanted to reconcile. I was so happy. They wanted my dad and me to come over to their house to talk things out. They answered the door together as a united front; their house had already been sprayed with a tension that hit me in the face. I was entering a hostile and doomed arbitration and I knew it. I felt that Mame had unintentionally set me up. As soon as we sat down, the accusations began to fly and I knew a horrible outcome was imminent.

They said I was the one who did drugs and I was the one who made the calls. They said these things with conviction and my theory that they actually believed it was even stronger. I expected my dad to turn on me and to try and strangle me. Instead, he devoutly defended me. Max scolded "You're always such a Martyr, Kathryn......" Me? I couldn't get a word in but was slapped in the face with this statement. It became an argument between my dad and Max while I stood there feeling helpless and Jessica#2 stood with her arms folded, indignant and satisfied. My dad became so upset that he started to hyperventilate. We decided to end it there and my dad and I went back to his house. I was furious with The Marvelous Mame and asked her not to ever try and fix my relationships again. She agreed that she wouldn't but her good heart wouldn't let her. For years, she tried to put in a good word for me with Kristen and James when she could. They haven't shown any interest to the point they made sure they didn't visit when I was in town.

For many years, my brother James and Kristen would each call when they knew I was in town and keep my dad on the phone for long periods of time making sure not to ask about me or even mention my name. I knew it was Kristen or James on the other end of the line because my dad seemed uncomfortable. Mame would later tell me that they only called and did this when I was in town. Were they marking their territory? Were they trying to hurt me? I don't know. In an apology letter I wrote to Kristen, I asked her if she would consider seeing me when I was in town for my dad's sake. I knew it would make him happy. I told her it didn't have to be any more than that. She never replied. James, however, is not only clever but has become an adept chiseler over the years. For a while, he came to visit when I was in town to ensure my dad's favor and it did. After James' translucent visits , my dad would praise him for coming over to "see me." My dad never noticed that James didn't talk to me, and when he looked at me, it was with cold, hateful eyes. He didn't notice that James monopolized his time and that his visits actually rubbed salt in my wounds.

The word "martyr" haunted me for years. Is that how Max saw me? Most people know nothing about my childhood. They don't know that I don't know my birth mother, I was raised by a complicated stepmother or that I have four siblings who have disowned me.

How could he see me as playing a martyr when it's his own mother whose life defines the very word? There are various definitions for this word but all of them concur that someone who plays the martyr seeks/expects recognition for suffering by creating drama. No, that would be Jade. Realizing that playing a martyr has a completely different meaning than actually being one dissolved this haunting. Of course Max "meant" that I was always playing the martyr but what he actually said was "you're always such a martyr." Albeit it was said in a sarcastic tone, I've decided to take it as a compliment after all these years.

An actual martyr is someone who has undergone severe or constant suffering and oh yes I certainly have. "Playing the martyr" would be if I continued to put myself in that position and let everyone know about my voluntary suffering. I no longer have the energy for people that don't find value in me. I don't even have the energy or time for people who don't bring me joy and frankly most of the people who have discarded me don't value me and/or no longer bring me joy.

Being cautious that anyone might ever think I am playing a martyr has made me adept at suffering in silence throughout my life. Unlike those people who tell you all their problems when you ask how they're doing. My response has been a pretty consistent, "I'm doing great! Thank you." I like that.

Sometimes when I came home from Africa or Europe as an adult, I would share stories about safari, a coup d'etat or the south of France and I could see a fog come over the minds of the people back home with whom I was actually trying to connect I wasn't boasting about my travels.

I was trying to share yet I still couldn't connect. My stories didn't resonate and I no longer felt like a match for Panama City. I know that most friends and family remained content in Panama City and few had traveled abroad. However, friends and family who stayed there had very full lives with long term friendships and rich family relationships that I could probably never understand.

I just wish I hadn't tried so hard to interest them with my stories from abroad. Once, Mame's daughter Gwen said, "I admire your life and fantasize about having lived abroad. I've never gone anywhere and I'm fascinated by your travels." I wanted to tell her how much I would have loved to stay dear friends with people from my childhood, my church, my family. I would have loved to have been able to have lunch with grade school friends and develop life long friendships with them. My moves and travels prevented me from having close relationships with my family and friends back home. Jade driving me away at the age of eighteen made me a perfect "out of sight, out of mind" target for the rest of the family to direct their own hurt and anger. I tried to tell her it was a trade off. I wanted to help her see the value and the beauty in the life she had chosen. I wanted to tell her I moved away because I was told I was a burden and a bastard but by moving away, I sacrificed any possibility of a relationship with Kristen and James. I had changed too much. Although I moved away due to Jade's persuasion, it had never occurred to me that leaving the panhandle would cost me so much. I also never imagined how far away I would actually go. My siblings seemed to grow increasingly jealous of my life abroad and the rip current of my travels pulled me further and further out to sea. In my dreams, I was being pulled out to sea and I desperately called out to them but they could no longer see or hear me.

Why does divorce have to be so ugly? I've seen what it's done to people and I've seen its devastation.

I didn't know that Jade was planning to file for divorce when she came to visit Max in Dallas many years before. Because I was still blind, I just remember being so excited to see her and to know he was visiting "us."

As silly as it might seem, I worked very hard to have what I had at the time. This was BEFORE I fortunately found myself in IT sales at just the right time. At this point I was still barley getting by. I was crazy in love with my little black cat, Abby. I found her in my flower garden outside my apartment. She was a tiny black cat with green eyes and she meowed constantly outside my door. I didn't have any money at the time and didn't think I could possibly take care of her so I called the Humane Society. They told me they could come and pick her up right away. I said, "Wait! What will they do with her when they come and get her?!" They said they would probably euthanize her. I didn't want her to die so I gave her what I intended to be a temporary abode. I took her to PetSmart and asked the staff to take her off my hands. The store politely declined and I came home with a shopping cart full of pet supplies and a tiny black cat that I couldn't afford to take care of. At this time when I felt so alone in the world, Abby became very precious to me and I believe she appeared in that garden especially for me. All I wanted was for Jade to come visit my apartment and to see Abby. I know it seems silly but I wanted Jade to take an interest in what was important to me. Instead, she flew into DFW and camped out at Max's house. I wanted her to see my apartment and meet my precious Abby. God, she seemed so selfish! She showed no desire to know anything about my life, to meet my cat, to see my apartment, to know about my job. I didn't see what I see now. She just didn't care about me at all.

Okay. With a little more love and compassion, maybe she was distraught about the upcoming divorce and was riddled with guilt about her affair. However, how many times over the years did she show no consideration for what was important to me? Time and time again. This was painful. How could she not see how painful this was to me? How could Max say that I was always playing the martyr when my feelings were so real?

I thought back to the ninth grade dance when I purchased my gown with babysitting money. It was an orange chiffon gown and I thought it was beautiful. In hindsight, I think it was heinous and wonder what in the world I was thinking. It was strapless and too big. Whoever I was "dancing" with had stepped on the hem. As we continued to "dance" around in circles, it took me a while to realize that my dress had turned around backwards. I had no breasts so it was relatively unnoticeable except to me.

Although I had witnessed the big deal that Jade made out of Max and Demi's school dances, it never once occurred to me that she didn't seem interested in mine. There were no planned pictures or corsages. Hell, I bought my own dress and she didn't even help me get it altered.

By my senior prom, I had grown into my orange chiffon dress from the ninth grade and thought it made sense to wear it again. It didn't need altering anymore and I had already paid for it. I went over to my friend Ashley's house to get ready for the prom. Her mom came into the room and gushed over Ashley's beauty. She was so emotional and in hindsight it was one of those beautiful mother/daughter moments that I allowed to resonate with me. It was lovely. It wasn't until many, many years later that I realized that my mom never once told me that I looked beautiful and as I grew older she NEVER bothered to take pictures. I wasn't beautiful to her, ever, and I knew it. I also knew that there is a beauty that mothers see in their own daughters that no one would ever see in me. I was a bastard and I was a flounder. I didn't have a mom to take me shopping for my dress or take pictures at my prom. Where was Jade when I was getting ready for the prom at Ashley's house, anyway? Where are all the pictures from my teenage years? "There never were any" is the answer.

There were Christmas ornaments though. We had each collected and made ornaments that had been saved in our Christmas boxes and brought out year after year. I had my favorites. I couldn't wait for Jade to bring them out each year and I would spend hours admiring them. Some had sentimental value because they had been given to me by special people; my most favorite was a cheerleader that was given to me at the football banquet in the fifth grade. Once, after Jade and my dad's divorce, Jade and I stopped by Demi's house. I noticed Demi's tree was decorated with all of the ornaments from our childhood except of course for the few that were representative of me, like the cheerleader. I can only try to express what I felt at that moment which was happy for Demi while somehow gutted that not one was saved for me, not even the ones Demi wouldn't have wanted. I can remember some of those ornaments in detail......the clown made out of Dixie cups.......How does Demi feel knowing she literally got everything; both the tangible and the invaluable.

In my twenties and thirties and forties, I noticed mothers and daughters shopping. I noticed them at lunch and at church and at weddings and baby showers. Sometimes I caught myself staring and had to consciously look away. It was fascinating to me. Every time I found myself in this trance watching them in wonder; I don't remember feeling anything except wonder. I didn't feel sad, suffering or like a martyr in any way. I found myself watching like a baby who sees himself in the mirror for the first time or the way I watch hummingbirds on those rare and quick sightings. One particular memory was a mom and daughter shopping. The mom begged her daughter to let her buy her a sweater. They giggled with comfort and ease like two best friends. I stared. The daughter told her mother that she was the one who needed a new sweater and they laughed even harder as if they had an inside joke. I was embarrassed to find myself staring and I didn't consider what or why I was feeling at the time. It was in hindsight that I realize it was just wonder. It wasn't self pity, it was just foreign to me. I had never laughed comfortably with Jade and never had her plead with me to buy me things.

When I married, I noticed the way my husband's mother doted on her only daughter. She told me a story about how her daughter had acne in college and she drove across the country to take her to a dermatologist as if it were an emergency. She told the story not as if it were an over-reaction but as if to her it really was an emergency. To me, it sounded ludicrous.

I remembered a time when my face broke out like a gazillion tiny volcanoes in high school. I worked in a department store when stone washed jeans came into fashion; finally I discovered this was an allergic reaction to the jeans. It was absolutely humiliating yet I dealt with it ON MY OWN. I continued to go to work sorting and selling stone washed jeans while my face itched, burned and oozed.

I also remember my reoccurring and excruciatingly painful ingrown toenails. I would dig down deep in my toes to extract the bloody jagged edges digging in my flesh and then pour hydrogen peroxide over them until they stopped fizzing. Several times I sprained my wrists trying to teach myself gymnastics and I self treated them because I knew Jade didn't care.

I never, ever once told Jade when my heart was broken from any of my many teenage disappointments. I suffered in silence with no one to console me but here's what's interesting and I hope comforting..........It's okay because I was looking up from the bottom with the two eyes on the top side of my flat body at the colorful symmetrical fishes swimming at the top and what I observed was lovely. Do you understand? BECAUSE I had no self pity, I was able to appreciate the beauty that would someday return to me.

My revelation was not going to be a sudden and seismic event. Instead it was a deep wound that had scabbed over and was eventually going to heal leaving me a scar that would remind me of what I've been through, how to treat others and how resilient I really am. The REASON this story is not in chronological order is deliberate.

Like a big, deep scab, in putting these memories to words, the scab has broken open, revealing past wounds that surfaced and bled a little here and there. A few times, that scab felt infected and I had to clean it and cover it for a while. I have a tiny scar on my hand where Abby snagged me while playing. I have another scar on my ankle where I hit a piece of coral snorkeling in the Indian Ocean with my husband and children. Scars tell our stories. The scars on my heart remind me that I am a survivor, that I worked hard for what I have, and that I have a full life of people who love me for me, just as I am.

Although I had comfortably grown warmer and warmer in that pot of increasingly hot water, and nearing 40 years of age, I finally decided to jump out after all. My children were very little and I didn't want them to be exposed to any type of poison; I finally saw Jade as toxic and poison TO ME. I also had experienced true, authentic love from flesh and blood, my own beautiful boys. I hope that Jade's relationship with Demi and Max is healthy and happy and that she isn't poison to them. Like an allergy, I decided she was something that was killing me. I had learned to love myself and I didn't want to have to perform a fake relationship with Jade for my children. Although I had kept coming back for bones for decades knowing I might get a bone or I might get kicked away, I finally realized I not only no longer needed those bones and that I didn't even desire them. Although I realize in that life I had been a flounder with two eyes on the top side of my head, I have now become one of the vibrant fish swimming merrily with the others at the top. I don't have to camouflage myself in the bottom of the sand anymore because Jade can't gig me, I have NO secrets or anything to be ashamed of. I haven't disowned her, I have set her free and coincidentally, I've set her free of me.

CHAPTER 26-FINDING MY TRUE MOM

I believe that having a mother is a birthright for most people yet there's a reason it wasn't for me and millions of others out there in the world. It wasn't part of our individual plans.

I have very deep friendships. I love my children so much my heart could explode.

If I could, I would adopt a million little girls and treat them like the precious treasures they are.

I don't know what jealousy or hatred feels like and I'm so grateful. I have never thought I was better than anyone. I didn't know I was attractive when heads turned when I walked in the door. It's funny that I didn't notice until I matured to an age where they stopped. This was a gift through my strange and corrupted normal.

All of the other people who have never felt the love of a mother, or have suffered any kind of abuse, I promise you it's a gift if we can just change our paradigm of thinking.

I have seen jealousy, hate, resentment and self entitlement up close and personal, especially in women. I'm so grateful to feel none of these things yet feel compassion for those who struggle with these emotions.

I've never been a daughter to a mother and I will never have a daughter. This is what I do have; I have two beautiful boys and I believe this was the design for this lifetime of mine and I am so grateful for it. I have grown to LOVE my yellow eyes, to tolerate my buck teeth and be proud I am a self made bastard, if indeed I am. See here's what's funny. The older I get, the more I look like my precious dad and I hear his laugh in my own laughter. I made my life what it is on my own without the help of a mother and that's okay. It's the journey that was designed for me and I finally embrace it with open arms.

Although, I didn't grow up to feel like a beloved daughter, I know what it feels like to be a beloved mother. My son, Bradley hugs me every day. He kisses me on the cheek or forehead and his love for me exudes. I have more than a handful of BEST friends and my oldest son has given me more laughter and joy in the sixteen years of his life than I have ever had in my life's entirety.

For so long, I couldn't understand why The Marvelous Miss Mame continued to force herself on me. I repeatedly told her that I didn't need a mom. I told her that I was happy she married my dad but asked her not to try to be my mom. She was relentless and it annoyed me. It annoyed me until the day, her powerful heart pierced through my resistance and I realized that she wasn't pushing herself on me for her interests. She was pushing herself on me for ME. She was going to give me a mom come "hell or high water." She didn't care if I was thirty years old. She thought I needed a mother and she wanted to give me a love that I had never known. When I come home, we go shopping and we fight over the check at lunch. We can talk about anything and everything and I can call her when my heart aches and she hurts with me. She cries when I arrive and when I leave. She is excited for my dad each chance he gets to go fishing and she sees the best in all of us; me, James and Kristen. She texts me everyday and if she doesn't hear from me for a few days, she worries. I have just recently started introducing her as simply "my mom" with no need to explain any more than that. Because she is.

That birthright to have a mom's love? Well, I've taken it back on my terms.

CHAPTER 27-LET IT BE

I've stopped hoping Kristen or James will be with Mame and my dad at the airport when I come to visit. I've stopped wishing they would come over to see me while I'm in town or call or send me a card for my birthday. It no longer hurts that they've taken no interest in my life or know my children. I've missed all of my nieces and nephews weddings because I wasn't invited and I'm over that too. For many years I felt sad as I was leaving Panama City because I knew the chance of seeing my siblings was over and it was always a let down. Instead now, my boys and I are loved by Mame's son and he treats me like a sister. Mame's daughters are kind to me and stop by to see me when their schedules allow. I'm still sad when I leave Panama City but now it's just because I have to leave my dad and my mom, Mame.

I was recently fact checking my story with my dad by very nervously reading it to him. I kept looking over to see if he had fallen asleep, looked bored, or angry by what I had written. He was just sitting there listening attentively. I gave him the opportunity to stop me at any point for corrections. Although he had absolutely no discrepancies, at some point afterward, he said, "You need to get Jade out of your head." What he doesn't understand is through telling this story, I have. I no longer have haunting dreams of her or of being in trouble. I no longer dream of Godzilla making me choose which siblings to stomp on. Instead, I dream of flying over beautiful landscapes and diving down and swimming with the beautiful tropical fish at the top of the water. I am no longer a stray dog begging her for a bone. I am no longer a frog slowly boiling to death in her pot and most of all, I am no longer a flounder.

I recently attended a funeral for a stranger with an elderly friend who desperately wanted to go but couldn't drive himself. She had chosen the songs and bible versus she wanted read at her funeral. ONE resonated with me, caused me to hold back tears and made me think about my life and my childhood. Out of all of my "churching," for whatever reason it felt as if I had never heard this verse before. I struggled with the "time to hate" as I have never hated anyone, ever. But I realized that I hate injustice, I hate prejudice, I hate judgement, I hate horn honking, bag pipes and holly bushes. Yes, there IS a time for hate. I realized that had not been for Jade, I would not have had so many of life's necessary experiences and challenges. It not had been for my observations and experience with prejudice, I might not understand it in a way that might help others understand it. If I had known I was decent looking or if I had been spoiled, I might have been vain. It not for all of these things, I may not have known that there is a time to embrace and a time to refrain, to search or to give up, to be silent or to speak. Jade taught me so such about life and I thank her, and I forgive her.

A Time for Everything- NIV

There is a time for everything,
and a season for every activity under the
heavens:
a time to be born and a time to die,
a time to plant and a time to uproot,
a time to kill and a time to heal,
a time to tear down and a time to build,
a time to weep and a time to laugh,
a time to mourn and a time to dance,
a time to scatter stones and a time to gather
them,
a time to embrace and a time to refrain from
embracing, a time to search and a time to give
up,
a time to keep and a time to throw away,
a time to tear and a time to mend,
a time to be silent and a time to speak,
a time to love and a time to hate,
a time for war and a time for peace.